Take a Lesbian to Lunch

CHARLOTTE FISHER

Author of
Mackinac Bridge Jesus

Forward

I am glad to write that a few of the following stories are no longer current due to the recent Supreme Court ruling making same-sex marriage legal across all 50 states and territories in the United States.

Writing for the majority, Justice Anthony Kennedy wrote, "It is now clear that the challenged laws burden the liberty of same-sex couples, and...they abridge central precepts of equality."

But while Justice Kennedy was writing on liberty and equality—aspects of American life we all cherish—others used the opportunity to escalate their war on gays. Justice Antonin Scalia wrote that the ruling was a threat to democracy. Louisiana Governor and presidential hopeful Bobby Jindal suggested getting rid of the court completely. Wisconsin Governor Scott Walker called for a constitutional amendment allowing states to define marriage as the union of one man and one woman. The Rev. Bill Owens, president of the Coalition of African-American Pastors, asked Christians to oppose the Supreme Court's gay marriage ruling through civil disobedience. He likened the decision to the error made in the Dred Scott case, saying, "The Supreme Court doesn't always get it right. This is one time they really got it wrong."

I wonder if the good Reverend can locate any references to "irony" in his bible.

And so the struggle for LGBT equality remains. In a recent op ed written for the Detroit Free Press, ACLU staff attorney Jay Kaplan outlined the many challenges still facing the LGBT community.

"In Michigan, the discriminatory adoption bill Governor Rick Snyder signed into law is part of a series of proposed legislation targeting the LGBT community. Our legislature has a number of bills in the pipeline, including a Senate-backed RFRA, which would permit individuals and businesses to openly discriminate against LGBT people in employment, housing and public accommodations.

"Other legislation would allow medical providers to refuse health services and gut local human-rights ordinances that protect the LGBT community from discrimination. All of these efforts are an attempt to deny LGBT people the same opportunities and dignity accorded to other Michigan residents."

Most important on Michigan's to-do list, says Kaplan, is amend our civil rights laws to include sexual orientation and gender identity as protected categories against discrimination.

In Michigan today, it is still legal to fire and deny LGBT people housing and public accommodations. While we can now be legally married, we can still be legally terminated by our employers when we return from our honeymoons. State Rep. Todd Courser (R-Lapeer) is proposing House Bills 4731, 4732 and 4733, which would require that all marriage certificates be signed by a religious leader, effectively taking the state out of the marriage business. He's also drafting legislation to ensure that religious leaders are not forced to perform marriages that go against their beliefs. It's a very transparent end-around to severely diminish the ability of same-sex couples to get legally married in Michigan. It demonstrates the length people will go to when motivated by fear and ignorance.

Let's not dilute ourselves into thinking that because of the SCOTUS ruling, full LGBT equality has been achieved. It hasn't. By a long shot. In fact, many believe the decision will galvanize the right's crusade to even more aggressively marginalize the LGBT community in our country. Texas and fistful of other petulant states are already defying the new marriage law of the land and thumbing their collective noses at the ruling.

John Culhane, writing for Politico Magazine, says, "In some ways, this new chapter of the gay marriage fight will likely mirror abortion rights in the wake of Roe v. Wade—a right technically legal but frustratingly difficult to exercise in many corners of the country. In many states, gay and lesbian couples will have great difficulty exercising their newfound marriage rights."

In his decision, Justice Kennedy wrote, "No union is more profound than marriage, for it embodies the highest ideals of love, fidelity, devotion, sacrifice and family. In forming a marital union, two people become something greater than they once were."

How can something conceived in love ignite such vitriolic hate? This is but another chapter in humankind's long-chronicled resistance to acceptance and change, played out in horror from Selma to Treblinka to Rwanda. Sometimes we get it right—14th Amendment to the U.S. Constitution—and sometimes we don't. Anti-gay Qatar, a lovely little country that deports, imprisons and kills its homosexuals, has been cleared to host the 2022 World Cup. I guess the U.S. women's soccer team will be staying home.

Still, it is a time for celebration. And a time to express our infinite gratitude to Supreme Court Justices Kennedy, Ruth Bader Ginsburg, Stephen G. Breyer, Sonia Sotomayor and Elena Kagan. Call me crazy, but I have hope left in this old heart. And, according to the late Mr. Steve Jobs, "The people who are crazy enough to think they can change the world are the ones who do."

Author

"Everyone is gay."
— *Kurt Cobain*

Stories

For My Beloved Redhead

My Big Fat Gay Ass

There are many predictions about the end of times. Some believe it will be marked by a specific event like the Battle of Armageddon.

I have my own Armageddon theory. I believe the end will be marked by a much more insidious conflict than the clash of good versus evil.

The final blow will come in a war between the fat and the thin.

Battle of the Bulge

Few things awaken our primal insecurities more than this epoch struggle. It threatens our moral compasses: what's right and wrong; what's good and bad; who's attractive and who's repulsive. Given the choice, who in their right mind would pick a best friend, spouse, physician, or even cleaning lady with a spare tire and double chin? We're a nation in love with Jack Sprat, but according to the latest statistics, are built like his wife and consumed with licking our enormous platters clean.

American obesity is at epidemic levels and is being faulted for astronomical healthcare costs, a declining GDP and a killing rate second only to tobacco. Former U.S. Surgeon General Richard Carmona once stated, "Obesity is a greater threat than terrorism." I guess I missed Kathleen Turner flying into a New York City skyscraper.

We are the fattest country on the planet. That we are also one of the richest, I guess, is just a coincidence. Michigan is one of the states with the heaviest populations. You can blame the weather, the auto industry, or all the fried perch dinners, but the result is the same. We're a mittenful of fat-assed, unemployed, sedentary people squeezed together on the couch eating Krispy Kreme doughnuts and watching the *The Biggest Loser.*

Throwing the weight of her office around, Michelle Obama is at war with the nation's girth, fighting a battle to shrink America's ever expanding bulge. She's even toppled the iconic food pyramid. Is that even in her job description? Despite her well-meaning words, even her husband was quoted saying, "You never want to get between Michelle and a tamale." I wonder who wears the snug-fitting pants in that family.

I don't care if the Obamas eat like Notorious B.I.G. or Jillian Michaels; just keep them away from my chicken pot pies. We conservatives want the White House to stay out of our kitchens: Focus on downsizing our government not our underwear.

Seriously, when the framers of our Constitution were grappling with big, heady issues like the balance between state and federal power, did they foresee a time when government would be legislating people's eating habits? In 1776, lard was one of the four basic food groups, along with headcheese, pickled tongue, and hard cider. Ben Franklin and Thomas Jefferson were hardly meeting at the Old City Tavern for tofu and fruit smoothies.

Three years after it banned smoking in restaurants, New York was the nation's first city to ban artery-clogging trans fats. No pastrami at Katz's deli? No cream cheese and lox? No knishes or egg creams or Nathan's Famous hot dogs? The decree left many clutching their chests in pain. Only in the U.S. can cigarettes and frying oils be both legal and illegal at the same time. Pretty soon it will be the death penalty for sugary soda refills and Super Big Gulps. When Congress goes after my salt shaker, I'm taking up arms.

Fat vs. Fiction

Who decides what's considered fat and what isn't? One day we're celebrating a look called heroin chic, the next we're criticizing Angelina Jolie for looking like a human skeleton. Why are we fixated with the ever-changing size of Jennifer Lopez's caboose? We idolize the girls on Project Runway and then ban overly thin models from top fashion shows. We want to eat our cake and throw it up, too.

The fashion industry has taken the hit for turning America's teens into neurotic waifs with eating disorders. Critics say the obsession with ultra-thinness has most girls and women hating their bodies. I don't buy into the feminist mantra that media hype alone creates objectification and dangerous eating habits. Any person—male or female—who's ever owned a mirror wants to be a built like a Greek god, and that's even before they watched the movie *300*. Correct body size—in most developed nations—equates to beauty, success, happiness and the most important of all inalienable rights—the right to have oodles of really great sex.

Had I been born 400 or so years earlier, my 25 excess pounds would have me scoring high on the sex-o-meter. Women labeled "rubenesque"—fleshy, well-fed women with swelling breasts and bouncy bellies—were all the rage in Peter the Great's day. Renaissance artists painted women with shameless layers of skin spilling off the canvas. *The Mona Lisa* was no Kate Moss.

Just a few decades ago, Jayne Mansfield and Marilyn Monroe were considered ideal beauties. Now we're rewriting history. At 140-pounds (her top weight), Marilyn would today be the target of every late-night comedian with a fat joke. Historians claim her measurements were 37-23-36: size 14 chest, size 6 waist and size 10 or 12 hips. By comparison, Natalie Portman—32A-24-33—weighs 105 pounds soaking wet. I could be wrong, but I bet they'll be selling pin-up posters of Marilyn long after Queen Amidala returns to Naboo.

So what are we? Overweight? Obese? Just plain fat? It seems today's obese was yesterday's pleasingly plump. Thanks to the World Health Organization, we have disparaging labels for the six subsets of human mass: underweight, normal weight, overweight, class I obesity, II and III. Other terms like severe, morbid and super morbid are also acceptable modifiers for people who fit into the last three categories, political correctness be damned.

According to most online body mass calculators, I am overweight. At my height (66 inches) I should weigh in at a skinny 123 pounds. I haven't been that light since I stopped snorting cocaine around the clock. Thankfully, that same website linked me to the South Beach Diet. Perhaps the calculator, advertisers and my former dope man are all in cahoots.

People try to hide their weight in embarrassing ways, giving such explanations as: "I'm a former athlete;" "I have a thyroid condition;" "I'm big boned;" "The camera adds 10 pounds;" "It runs in the family." At 300 pounds, I doubt anyone runs in that family.

A friend of mine recently sent me one of those "People of Walmart" photo collections. A class III obese woman was photographed lifting her enormous body out of her Go-Go Scooter 5000, reaching for a bottle of no-brand vodka on the upper-most shelf. In the next frame, she was captured on her tippy toes, clutching the booze with great pride. Who says there are no modern-day miracles? When you've taken to wearing kaftans and you're not Islamic, you might want to consider a Lap Band.

The Food Channel Made Me Do It

Star magazine's best-selling issue features "The 45 Best and Worst Beach Bodies" and shows celebrity photos of sun-kissed beauties and Hollywood's unfortunate beasts. Does anyone really want to see Gerard Depardieu in a Speedo? Tori Spelling was photographed looking like the Scarecrow with enormous boobs. I don't want to see Mischa's cellulite, Britney's butt, or Kelly Osbourne's silicone cups running over.

Who do we worship? Kirstie Alley or Ally McBeal? Neither, actually. The newest "in" personality is the celebrity chef. These folks walked out from behind the chopping block onto the red carpet and are packing a powerful paczki. Emeril Lagasse—with restaurants, TV shows, and branded merchandise like cookware, signature spices, books, music, tableware, apparel and specialty food delivered to your front door—can practically buy and sell Donald Trump. Rachel Ray is bigger than the Holy Roman Empire. Bobby Flay, the freckle-faced Howdy Doody look alike, is a rock star. He's hotter than A-Rod and P Diddy combined. His wife, Stephanie March, is so undeniably out of his league she must have a BBQ addiction. This guy probably got beat up at school for packing watercress finger sandwiches in a Julia Child lunchbox and garnishing his Halloween candy.

Celebrity chefs are the Pied Pipers of Chubby Town. Not a one got famous for serving boiled Brussels sprouts. Lagasse thinks bread pudding with bourbon sauce is a breakfast cereal. He developed a recipe for candied bacon. You've got to love a guy whose catch phrase is, "Pork fat rules."

Are we celebrating the lean or the cuisine? Adam Richman hosts The Travel Channel's "Man v. Food," a show dedicated to eating your body weight in meat. The young man goes from town to town in an attempt to eat America. In Tucson, he ate a hamburger comprised of 12 patties, 12 slices of cheese, and all the fixings—in less than twenty minutes. He's wolfed down a 3 meter bratwurst, a 7 pound breakfast burrito and 15 dozen oysters in mere minutes. After eating a 48 ounce porterhouse steak in less time than it takes to sing the national anthem, Richman delivered his delicious catch phrase, "In the battle of man versus food, today man won."

So did his cardiologist.

Everything related to food is now decorated, celebrated and priced out of orbit. Friends of ours received an Le Creuset Enameled Cast Iron French Oven as a wedding gift that cost more than my first car. Williams Sonoma sells a truffle finishing sauce priced at $23 for a 12 ounce bottle. If I'm spending that kind of dough on a bottle, it better be 151 proof.

Growing up, my mom bought her pots and pans at Kmart, finished her roasts with pan gravy, and bought seasonally available fruit at Jerry's farm market down the street—apples in fall, cherries in summer, canned peaches in heavy syrup in the dead of winter.

Then again, no one had yet come up with a recipe for deep-fried Thanksgiving turkeys or waffle cones made with bacon.

Move Over, Richard Simmons

In addition to *The Biggest Loser*, there are tons of other weight-loss based reality shows airing including *Dance Your Ass Off*; *Supersize vs. Superskinny*; *Honey, We're Killing the Kids*; *X-Weighted* and *Fat Chef.* I'm intrigued by a show titled *Shedding for the Wedding.* The competition forces couples to lose weight and at the same time plan for matrimonial bliss.

When contestants aren't engaged in endless hours of grueling workouts, they're planning their wedding. After just two days with both a personal trainer and wedding planner, I'd be up on double homicide charges, which would undoubtedly be great for ratings.

Critics say overly restrictive diets and injury-provoking exercise can be hazardous to one's health. In a span of just 16 minutes, three men dropped dead while running the 2009 *Detroit Free Press/Flagstar* Half Marathon. In comparison, no one has ever died in our neighborhood Hostess Bake Shop Outlet—not even on Twinkie Tuesday.

Super Size Me

What should we be eating? Mediterraneans' suggest a liquid diet of olive oil and red wine. The northern

Chinese bank on noodles, pancakes, and dumplings cooked in generous amounts of salt and fat. Like religion, we all subscribe to a different food theology. Some nutrition experts, likely bankrolled by Hershey lobbyists, say dark chocolate prevents cancer and wards off dementia. Other experts claim beer improves cardiovascular function, eggs reduce cholesterol and butter enhances the immune system. My grandmother began every dish—even a dinner salad—by rendering a pound of well-marbled pork. She lived an active, healthy life for more than 93 years.

In the movie *Super Size Me*, filmmaker Morgan Spurlock ate at McDonald's—breakfast, lunch and dinner—exclusively for 30 days. He gained nearly 25 pounds, in addition to experiencing mood swings and sexual dysfunction. In all fairness, I think it's hard to orgasm while sucking on a Shamrock Shake.

This made for great cinema—a defenseless David versus a force-feeding Goliath—and erased any sense of personal responsibility we have for ordering the "two apple pies for $1.00" option off the extra value menu. After the film's release, a number of people came forth with contrary claims, stating that an exclusive Golden Arches diet was a sure way to lose weight.

Who do you believe?

Only the Hamburgler knows for sure.

So much for comfort food being comfortable. Every nutrition label in the grocery store looks like a pirate flag. When did an 8-ounce bag of Tostitos turn into 14 servings? Do I really want to know how many fat grams are contained in a Peanut Buster Parfait? Are veggie burgers, veggie bacon and veggie ribs really considered meat substitutes? And what the hell makes them taste like farm animals?

Skinny Bitch

This is what captures headlines today: Judge strips taco-eating Texas beauty queen of crown.

Stop the presses.

The title of Miss San Antonio was removed from 17-year-old Domonique Ramirez and passed to her slimmer runner-up because contest sponsors accused her of eating "too many tacos." Apparently a clause in the contract required the 129 pound Ramirez to stay that weight for one full year.

Seems like the real victims here are the tacos.

This is just one example of what is being described as fat discrimination. Historians claim the practice began in the 1960s, when—while most normal hippies were protesting the Vietnam War by having free sex and smoking dope—the first fat activists were eating ice cream while burning posters of the über-thin model Twiggy.

Isn't "fat activist" an oxymoron?

According to these plus-sized naysayers, the "obesity pandemic" is a hoax drumsticked up by those with the most to gain—namely the weight loss industry, estimated at an annual $100 billion in the U.S. alone.

They claim this "fear of fat" that's spreading like Philadelphia Cream Cheese across the land is nothing more than shame-based hyperbole.

Linda Bacon (does anyone else smell the irony here) is author of *Health at Every Size*. She claims that fat people face discrimination in all areas of life, from squeezing into tiny airplane seats to buying new clothes off the rack. Bacon says that fat bias operates as the last acceptable form of discrimination and is more prevalent than discrimination based on race or gender.

She also claims that there's a lot of cultural support for fat oppression and that thinner folks are given more privilege in the world. Really? Has she ever heard of CeeLo Green, Brian Wilson, Pavarotti or Meatloaf?

Though I'm no expert, I'd have to disagree with Ms. Bacon. If I were the size of a grand piano, I doubt I'd find anything to be happy about, even a discrimination-free world. Proof positive: Media mogul Oprah is as popular wearing size 8 jeans as she is the size of a Fiat 500. Her bank account grows regardless of what her scale says.

Equal Opportunity Discrimination

There are people who believe if we simply get rid of all the blacks or Muslims or gays or now the fat asses, everything in the world will finally be perfect. God knows we'd all be better off with a few less people needing a little more room

11

Unfortunately, things are rarely that cut and dried. If we disposed of all the Paul Prudhommes and Mario Batalis, where would we be? Who'd cook Sunday brunch? Isn't it the fat guy or gal who makes us laugh the hardest—the funny fluffies like Whoppi Goldberg, John Candy and Garfield? Who is Fat Albert without his loveable love handles? Was Karen Carpenter's tune that much sweeter than Mama Cass'? Would Hattie McDaniel's Mammy have worked as a dainty size two? Has anyone ever seen an anorexic opera singer? Were Brando and Elvis bigger when they were smaller? And what about the man with the little round belly that shakes when he laughs like a bowl full of jelly?

Pound for pound, is Barack Obama a better president than Bill Clinton or William Howard Taft?

Weighing in on the topic, Dr. David Katz, director of the Yale-Griffin Hospital Prevention Research Center, is quoted saying, "Food is potentially the best medicine there is."

If that's the case, I'll take a pizza calzone, a bowl of chicken gravy and a Sanders hot fudge cream puff. But hold the nuts—I read someplace they're fattening.

TLL

Bully

A friend's 12 year old son called her from inside his school locker earlier in the week. Apparently, the resident bully thought it would be big fun to stuff Luke in there and the rest of the class agreed. I don't know all the specifics. It was certainly no Columbine, but it did not sound good. People, regardless how small they are, shouldn't been treated like carry-on luggage.

The remainder of the week Luke fabricated an illness to avoid reliving the humiliation.

Luke's story awakened my own memories of being bullied: Denied service at a fast-food restaurant for being gay; shamed in the school lunchroom for my blood-sausage sandwich; mercilessly mocked for my Bjorn Borg hairdo. Okay, I deserved that last one.

My feelings of disgrace were not unique. Upon hearing the tale, everyone in my recovery circle cringed at their own indelible bully moment, including Luke's mother Liz. It seemed this young boy tapped into a palpable wound that for each of us still wept.

Together, we shared our war stories: The kid who stole our lunch money; the dad who beat us for walking away from a fight; the brother who humiliated us for wetting the bed; the mother who withheld her love.

A few of us admitted that we ourselves were the bullies. I called one of my school mates "half-pint" because she dressed like Melissa Gilbert on *Little House on the Prairie*. One man forced his smarter, weaker sibling to do his homework, threatening to beat him in ways that left no tell-tale marks. This guy had done prison time, I didn't ask for details.

Some in our group, men and women ranging from 17 to 70, left the meeting in tears, not just for the boy in the locker, but for their residual rage and shame. The topic became a powder keg igniting the memories of all the shitty things that had ever been done to us, along with the injustice, hatred and ignorance that still exists.

Above it all, was the overwhelming feeling of powerlessness. For an alcoholic in recovery, powerlessness is as basic as it gets.

Abuse of power sucks, especially ugly at Luke's tender age, when kids are trying to find their place in the world. Who knows how the locker incident will imprint Luke's subconscious? Maybe he'll understand himself to be a bad person who deserves bad things. Maybe he'll become an arsenal of rage, stockpiling his anger and releasing it on a future wife or child. Maybe he'll withdraw altogether, choosing isolation as a safe haven against society. Or maybe he'll use the experience to fight tyranny and give a voice to those who would otherwise have none. I guess only Luke will decide how this hateful incident will play out.

We told Liz her actions will likely leave as big a mark on her son as the bully's, hopefully helping Luke to learn healing and forgiveness. That she did not want to hear. Who wants to be a model for good behavior when your son has been violated?

Liz, a feisty red head, had 14 months in recovery at the time of the incident and a temper like a feral cat. This is a woman who used to start bar fights and whom I suspect won more than her share. The locker incident unleashed her non-sober beast. She talked of waging an apocalyptic war on the school administration, the bully's parents, the state of Michigan and any poor slob within three-square-miles of her son's locker.

"It's my job to keep him safe," she wept. "What the hell good is being sober if I'm still powerless?"

Animal mothers—bears, geese, hamsters—kill anything that threatens their young. It's Mother Nature's number one law. Yet we sober humans are yoked with the responsibility of exercising restraint and practicing good behavior. It isn't acceptable for us to go all "Discovery Channel" on someone in our tame society, regardless the circumstances. Maybe Mother Nature has it right. I'm quite sure that if Simba's mother had received a call from her cub's locker, that bully would have been dealt with swiftly, decisively and then served for supper with pride.

In This Corner Wearing Red Trunks

The happy ending to this story—aside from the bully getting suspended and the school adopting an anti-bullying program—is that Liz had a real growth moment. What she *wanted* to do (see above Discovery Channel reference) was not what she actually *did* (model impeccable behavior). She took that half-second between impulse and action to stop and think—and pray—about her next move. She played the tape of her old irrational behavior and chose not to repeat the pattern. Liz did something few of us ever do; change. I call that progress of the first order. Some might even call it a miracle.

Who's Your Bully?

Why do people abuse power? The same reason a dog licks his balls.

I'm sure there are many theories on what motivates bullies. Many people agree that bullies were or are themselves victims of violence and harassment. Others conclude that bullies are driven by fear. The bullies I've known are afraid of losing something they think they have (safety, security, power, status) or not getting something they think they deserve (unbridled adoration).

Bullies often have a flawed sense of justice. The extreme Christian Right, for example, really believes that gays—allowed to live unchecked in society—will destroy God's plan. If they don't stamp out homosexuality, they will have literal hell to pay. Their fury is visceral, same as a mother bear. They act without fear of reprisal or death. They are social terrorists.

Unfortunately, bullies come in all shapes and sizes, like Charles Atlas' muscle-bound boor who kicks sand in the face of the 100 pound weakling. Bullies are the guys in movies—like *Beauty and the Beast*'s Gaston—who stomp around wearing muddy boots and yell for people to get them beer and attend to their narcissism. The Biff Tannens (*Back to the Future*) and Nelson Munzs (*The Simpsons*) of the world take your new *Peanuts* pencil pouch, give you a dumb nickname (Char-lot-fart-a-lot) and send you home from school with a super-atomic wedgie.

While cute as kids, they can grow up to be toxic megalomaniacs—the likes of Adolph Hitler, Saddam Hussein and Omar al-Bashir. This class of pathological bully shocks our sensibility with horrors like Buchenwald, Rwanda and Bosnia.

Still other bullies parade as your neighbor, priest, congressman and network news anchor. They threaten that praying to the wrong god will lead to your eternal damnation. They rape corporations, crush families and decimate small towns. They tell small businessmen how much profit is too much. They call you unpatriotic because you oppose a war, or an "angry mob" when expressing your First Amendment rights. They wear slick suits and speak eloquently. They own the bully pulpit. They buy themselves private islands and gold-plated 9 irons.

Grown Up Bullies

Many of my bully moments have come later in life when logic suggests I should have known better how to handle life's thugs. Not this girl. I'm still an easy target for people whose motive it is to cause me fear, embarrassment and a general sense of helplessness.

I don't think I've ever handled a bully moment well. I've never delivered a comeuppance that sent a nasty brute away in tears. Maybe that's why bullies are so good at what they do—they rarely face an equal opponent.

One Under Every Rock

I'm not proud to say I've been bullied by all sorts of people, including one man who thought he could have sex with me because he was president of the local union and I was 23.

One boss embarrassed and intimidated me in every conceivable way. I think she did it for sport. I took shots for being gay, having an intermittent stutter and wearing a little black beret my best friend bought for me in Paris. By the time this bully fired me, I had begun believing her opinion of me. And peeing submissively.

More often than not I've been the bully, which is possibly an even crummier role than being the victim. It horrifies me to know how I can degrade people to feed

18

my diseased ego. Being aware that I have the capacity to both wound and be wounded is an important realization.

Abuse is a vicious circle. My dad was physically violent with me, and I've been abusive with others. He abused booze and I repeated the cycle. He bullied me and I bullied myself.

Mean People Suck

My father was a first-class bully. I have hundreds of gut-wrenching tales of a young Charlotte being emotionally and physically abused by this alcoholic mad man. I bring them out like fine china when I host myself a pity party. Two particular stories I keep close at hand in case of emergencies.

Act 1

Toward the end of my sophomore year at Michigan State University, I was encouraged by the university to declare a major. I had been focusing all my energy in the music department. Truth be told, I had been focusing all my energy in the bars. Anyway, my father called me home in a very Marlon Brandon cum Vito Corleone way to discuss my options.

My dad and I didn't have discussions, if your definition of a discussion is: one person talks, the other person listens, waits for them to finish, reflects on what was said and repeats the process. No. My dad lectured, demanded, threatened and then threw in a pinch of criticism for his own amusement. I usually held my breath, turned red, cried and then got high. We could have used a bit of coaching on our communications skills.

My dad's message was clear: Under no circumstances would he continue helping to fund my education if I chose music as my major. He said that after four years of school I needed to graduate in a field that would be economically self-sustaining—something where I could make a decent living. He was sure that wasn't a career in music.

"I'm not supporting you for the rest of your life," he said ominously. "You're not coming back home for any more free lunches."

We agreed instead that I would become—here's the big joke—a Journalism major. My first full-time journalism job paid $12,000 a year.

Sadly I haven't played the drums in nearly 20 years. It's caused me great sadness. I still I tear up at parades, football games and at the mention of John Philip Sousa.

Act 2

My other favorite bully story explains precisely how my dad ruined the rest of my life. Again, I was at MSU, but this event occurred during my freshman year.

I was head-over-heels in love. I met Robin in high school. She was a majorette and a year my junior. She wore a sequin bodysuit and twirled fire. I never had a chance. When I left for college, we connived to spend every possible moment together, devising a million schemes to conceal our forbidden love.

To our naïve surprise, our subterfuge did not work. Even though we didn't date boys, had lots of sleepovers together, and a wardrobe rich in flannel, people started getting suspicious. Especially my dad. He was going to nip this thing in the bud.

I was summoned home from East Lansing aboard a Greyhound to the slaughterhouse of my father's den. I would take the seat between my mother and father's twin La-Z-Boy thrones.

My father took a deep drag on his unfiltered cigarette and exhaled slowly.

"Your mother and I believe there's something unholy going on between you and Robin," he said. "If that is indeed the case, you are no longer part of this family."

Unholy? This, from the man who taught us to lie about attending Sunday mass.

My mother nodded in agreement, knowing to do otherwise would slit her own throat.

Pathetically and without hesitation, I denied the accusation, fabricating lie upon lie to explain away the obvious signs of our lesbian relationship.

The accusation drove Robin and me deeper into hiding. She and I would continue to be closeted together in a tormented relationship for another five years before she dumped me and married a man. It was the perfect ending. Shakespeare himself could not have scripted a more tragic tale.

The abandonment—real and threatened—and shame of my perceived sexual aberration fueled my addiction. I dove deeper into drugs and booze and—in yet another example of insanity—I also married, providing my parents the perfect son-in-law.

In conclusion, that's how my dad ruined my life.

As a side note, my dad had made a similar threat to my sister four-and-a-half years earlier. Her sin was seeing a young *man* dad judged not appropriate. Our father tried everything to tear the young couple apart, eventually delivering the same ultimatum: "Stop seeing him or I'm kicking you out of the house."

God bless her, my sister didn't so much as blink. One "Fuck you" later and dad was packing her every belonging in our 1969 Plymouth Barracuda and screaming like a major-league umpire, "You're out."

She had—for once—put the bully in his place.

Thank You Notes

Bullies have played an important role in my addiction and self-destruction. They've allowed me to stay stuck. To quit on myself. And hide.

In his book *Excuses Begone*, Dr. Wayne Dyer lists 18 common excuses people use to explain away an unhappy existence. I needed only one; my dad. I used him over and over to deflect owning my miserable life.

When I look back at my teens, I wonder what would have happened had I not used his intimidation as an excuse. Would I have been brave enough to try? And if I failed, who would I have blamed?

Because of my dad, I convinced myself, I was robbed. I gave him all the power necessary to stay safely in my pain and cowardice.

He was the perfect bully. He was my perfect excuse. And then he died.

Bitter, Party of One

I was sober more than two years when my dad passed away. We left each other on not the greatest of terms. I spent many hours on my therapist's couch raging and blaming. I was jeopardizing my recovery.

Over time, she helped me release my dad from my prison of hatred.

Without Dad as an alibi, I very slowly began to accept responsibility for the choices I made. I then took all my misdirected anger and turned it inward—as alcoholics like to do.

"Why couldn't I have been more like my sister?" I ranted. She was brave. She had conviction. She left home with my dad's crappy used car while I stood mute, without a scrap of dignity and in time inherited his AMC Concord.

But shifting the hate didn't work for me, either.

I had to accept life without blame.

Happy Days

I've come to the conclusion that my dad was the way he was, simply because that's the way he was.

I don't think he laid awake nights thinking up new ways to make his family's lives miserable. I'm almost certain what he did he did out of love, with the tools available for dads in the 60s and 70s. My alcoholic father was raised by his alcoholic father and co-dependent mom, who believed they were doing the Lord's work. My grandparents walked a very narrow path of religious righteousness and beat the shit out of their kids if they fell off their limited interpretation of God's beam.

Funny how the cycle repeats itself.

My dad became a dad without the skills to father two daughters who saw for themselves very different lives than was outlined in his plan. No doubt, his singular objective was to keep us safe. From menacing low-life, motorcycle-driving steel workers and lesbians and the depravity of life as a musician. But as every dad eventually learns, you can't keep your children safe. And you can't keep them from their lives.

Be Not Afraid

In the end, it is said, there is only fear and love. My dad's fears were epic—safety, security, rejection, damnation, powerlessness. And I inherited every one.

But I'm also willing to believe there is love.

Like Luke's mom, I have the power to change and start practicing something called forgiveness. I usually reserve forgiveness for people who actually ask for it. Even then it can be hard. But I can't make that a condition. The people who don't want it are often the ones who need it most. Like me.

Today I'm making a new choice. With every bully I meet, I will offer them up to God, turn the other cheek and look for the Christ in their troubled hearts. If I don't, my very human self will push them into an open manhole cover, which is not very spiritual. I can't be joyous and free if I'm engaged in nonsense. Like my good friend Dave says, "It's not a tennis match if you don't hit the ball back."

If, like Liz, I model good behavior, maybe all the bullies will go home and take their hate with them. Maybe if enough of us don't hit the ball back, they'll stop looking for a game. That's all I can really hope for.

That and a set of bongos.

TLL

Help

Rarely do the worlds of my two favorite Sharons (one straight BFF, one lesbian life partner) collide. It's not as if they appeared in the same photograph our universe would implode. They don't dislike each other; there is no acrimony. We just have a very formal and separate recognition of church and state. The BFF is all church. We talk about spirituality, sure, but so much more. Like the stuff that happened before the other Sharon was born. And people who dress funny.

The Sharon I sleep with is much more serious and redder headed. She could be a head of state. She wears the demeanor of gravitas. She may actually be too bright for her—and my—own good.

So on the occasion that they—independently—insert into conversations with me the same topic, I consider it either legitimately weighty or paranormal.

Such was the case with PPO—Person-to-Person Outsourcing—a subject with which I was neither familiar nor interested. To have the topic introduced twice was surreal and redundantly annoying.

The BFF is an avid listener of National Public Radio. She gets her best material quoting *All Things Considered* and the *Diane Rehm Show*. That, and the *New York*

Times. I warn her if she leans any more to the left she'll fall off the edge of the earth. It was in the course of spewing her liberal propaganda that she referenced the newly coined term, Personal Outsourcing.

My Woman in Tokyo

Here's what I understood her to say: Just like the greedy multinational corporations have been doing for years, individuals can now farm out their unwanted work cheaply. Obscenely cheaply. And yes, the country gaining most from our employment out-basket is India.

No off-shored tasks are off limits. PPO is outsourcing at the micro level—administrative support, IT, marketing, tutoring, accounting, editorial writing and graphic design. Websites such as outsource2india.com and yourmaninindia.com can hook you up with eager and brilliant minds who'd like nothing better than to balance your check book and write your daughter's college entrance essay for a fraction of minimum wage and with no healthcare benefits required.

According to news reports, person-to-person outsourcing is already generating global revenue of $250 million annually and is expected to hit $2 billion soon.

What started simply as a type of concierge service to assist Indian ex-pats with their left-behind obligations—bills, household tasks, aging parents—has turned into a full-blown Kelly Service for every American honey-do task imaginable.

BFF Sharon found this development fascinating. She was high on the fantasy of farming out limitless tasks to faceless brown-skinned 20-somethings. I had to repeatedly remind her that she could not outsource her child rearing to Bangalore.

With this discussion still fresh on my tongue, the red-headed Sharon—out of the blue—began a like conversation. How outsourcing our most menial tasks to some poor "Peggy" in India would make our lives better—more efficient and far superior. As with straight Sharon, I reminded young Sharon that we could not outsource our pet rearing to Mumbai. An even worse outcome could prevail.

Red Sharon (as in state, not square) plucked her understanding of PPO from Timothy Ferriss' popular book, *The 4-Hour Workweek*. In his best seller, Tim unlocks the secret to occupational efficiency and boils it down to the time it takes to shave my legs. "Personal outsourcing" is just one of the many plums Sharon picked from Ferriss, who's gone on to write *The 4-Hour Body* and *The 4-Hour Chef*. His literary propagation leads me to believe Mr. Ferriss has more than one off-shore wordsmith cranking out his four-hour copy.

Throughout time, we humans have made it our quest to design and build a better mouse trap. Tim's version includes the compression of time. If we can simply condense work (or exercise or food preparation) into an intensely potent four-hour dose—an effusive concentration of its former self—we can redirect our remaining hours in more meaningful ways. As imagined on Ferriss' book cover, that higher calling has something to do with palm trees and hammocks. Just as God intended, I'm sure.

Personal outsourcing is a wave not likely to wane, especially with blog post testimonials like this: "I've got a guy in India. He is intelligent, dependable, creative and witty. He works 24/7 and never gives me excuses. He is an MBA. He is a CPA. He is a PhD. Basically there is no subject matter he has not mastered."

I'm sure this guy is worth his weight in saffron. Had I an extra $4/hour for payroll, the dimly amusing words you're reading right now would have been written by my own private cut-rate Patel.

I don't begrudge a startup company the right to hire a gal Friday on the Asian continent. If an ingenious entrepreneur can get tech support and bookkeeping for rupees on the dollar, I say, "Hooray." I fully support capitalism and global economic competition. After all, it's just business.

What I can't support is using people—any people—like underpaid pack mules. Tasks that are personal, done without the intervention of another person, should remain that way, Hindu, Buddhist or otherwise. I don't care if you're Donald Trump or Warren Buffett, do you really need an army of overseas minions to book your tee times and order your monogrammed cocktail napkins? I'm certainly not important enough to outsource anything to anyone. Honestly, I'm embarrassed to do most of my own work.

An *Esquire* editor wrote a tongue-in-cheek blog about his own experience with PPO. His Indian support team helped find his son a Tickle-Me-Elmo doll for Christmas, correct an erroneous credit card bill, and locate an affordable cell phone plan for his family. They even sent an "Apology" bouquet to the editor's wife after a particularly nasty dispute. Nothing says "I'm Sorry" like posies from Ahmedabad.

Outsourced, Mississippi

You need not visit Delhi to see this commerce in practice.

Kathryn Stockett's wildly popular book, *The Help*, is yet another adaptation of how we live productive lives thanks to the endless efforts of a supporting cast. Apparently in 1962 Mississippi, it was both fashionable and compulsory to employ help. Mothers—young and old—entrusted the family enterprise to a host of caregivers with whom they wouldn't share their indoor plumbing. It was unclear to me—in both the novel and the movie—why these women needed so much assistance. They did not work outside the home, did not produce an inordinate number of offspring, and did not live without modern conveniences like the electric light or garbage disposals. And yet they all had maids. Perhaps employing help was a cultural norm, handed down from generation to generation like good linen and family bibles. Maybe it was an economic expectation—bragging rights for those with proper street addresses and framed college diplomas. Whatever the reason, those impotent women lived behind a very thin mask of perfection. Many were fragile, ignorant, and ready to collapse at the first sign of messy diapers and dirty dishes. They suffered a poverty of enlightenment.

Whatever the case, the maids of *The Help* were the mortar of the family home. They gave their lives in devotion to children not of their womb or skin color.

Growing up, I didn't know a single family that had *help*. Then again, I was born in 1963, north of the Mason-Dixon Line. Had we the money, I'm sure my mother would have loved outsourcing what little housework she did to a crisply-starched maid. That would have freed her to fully dedicate herself to soap operas and prescription pills without interruption.

Today, the cycle has come full circle. Instead of African-American caretakers tending to the one-percent's offspring, they are instead tending to the one-percent. Yes, wealthy Jews and gentiles no longer in command of their bladders are dependent on new millennium Minnys. Nearly a half-century after the Selma marches, black women in white uniforms still ride busses from inner cities to elaborately preened suburbs to feed, dress and wipe the infirm asses of millionaires no longer capable of chewing their own food. Without LaTasesha and Moesha, neither Kirk Kerkorian nor David Rockefeller, Sr., would have matching shoes on their feet, not to mention their false teeth. They may be flush with cash, but without help, these nonagenarians aren't even able to flush.

From Riches to Rags

I never had the kind of millionaire lifestyle vilified by Barack Obama in his war on wealth. I never had a private jet, nor did I light Cuban cigars with newly minted $100 bills.

But despite never having been in the top bracket of America's money holders, I always seemed to have a lot of help. Maybe not in a Mitt "employed illegal immigrants to do lawn work at his Massachusetts Belmont home" type. And certainly not Arnold's "fathered a love child with a long-time member of his household staff" kind. But definitely in a "have a drink, make a phone call, write a check" kind of help. "Put my VISA number on file and take care of it" kind of help. "Just shut my bedroom door quietly and handle it" kind of help.

I needed a lot of help. And I got it.

Over the years my life has resembled Cinderella preparing for the ball—lots of fat little mice and bluebirds arranging my chaotic shit for appearance sake. Those helpers kept my magical fantasy alive when I no longer could.

The list of people in my past employ is long and—depending on your perspective—impressive or pathetic. I've had personal shoppers, dog walkers, lawn

32

maintenance crews (quite likely undocumented aliens), house cleaners, decorators, fitness trainers, drug dealers, personal chefs, party planners, gift shoppers, money managers and people who delivered me shiny new cars on a frequent basis.

I even had a sympathetic therapist listen to me moan about how terribly difficult it all was.

The more I drank, the more elaborate my outsourcing became. "We really need someone to decorate our house for Christmas?" my ex-husband would ask. "Who is this guy Kyle and why is he arranging my closet?" Help was not part of his family's DNA. If there was something to be done, he did it. Even if he did it badly, which he did not.

Other than my ex-husband, everyone else seemed happy with the arrangement. The baby showers went off without a hitch, the vacations were sheer perfection, and every holiday was a Rockwell painting. Or so I was told.

I once paid a woman $100 to give me a bath. I was living in Japan. She filled the tub with foamy water and aromatics. She sponged me suggestively and massaged my bare shoulders with her small, delicate hands. She even patted me dry, dabbing me with warm, thirsty towels. I'm sure I would have paid her double had she joined me with her rubber ducky.

Help! I Need Somebody!

Maybe this behavior isn't extraordinary for modern middle-class America. Maybe "help" is how we all get by—that and unlimited refills of Adderall. In fact, "help" continues to be a status symbol, like designer dogs and phones smart enough to land a space shuttle. We hoist ourselves on the shoulders of our Indian Peggys to claim freedom from the rat race and proclaim economic superiority.

And then one day we realize our lives are no longer our own.

At some point during my active addiction I stopped being personally engaged in my own life. I made certain (most) everything got done, but without getting my hands dirty. I just couldn't bother being bothered. About the only thing I did myself was make drinks and buy drugs. That was exhausting enough.

Today the economics of my life have changed dramatically. Divorce and job loss can do that to a person. Gone are the endless streams of smiling uniformed people delivering fresh laundry, Artesian water and Russian vodka to the back door. I miss my helpers, who whistled while they worked and I napped.

Unfortunately, I get little consolation from my newfound friends in recovery. I receive no comfort when I complain about car insurance or dog groomers or the smell of my five year old SUV. Even after several years of continuous sobriety, I have not reclaimed my former position of prosperity. A life of financial bliss remains elusive. In fact, you could call my situation a textbook reversal of fortune.

Brother, Can You Spare a Dime?

I once had *help*.

I now am *help*.

Not in an Aibileen way. No one I know is crazy enough to give me responsibility for their children or the cakes for their Junior League teas. But I am help in the classic sense. I do those things I once thought menial and beneath me, and I'm doing those things for others as well.

Today I have dirt under my nails and dog poop in the treads of my sneakers. It doesn't make me better than anyone else. It just feels good to finally connect with my own life—to know how much money is in my bank account and what exactly is growing in my refrigerator. I water my flowers. I gas up my car and buy vacuum cleaner bags and clean litter boxes from dawn until dusk.

In fact, I have become somewhat of an entrepreneur in the house-pet industry, providing a variety of services for domesticated animals. The people who hire me love their pets. And since I love their pets, they've grown to love me. Really love me, as in buy me Christmas presents and send me their vacation photos.

I have gone full circle in the pecking order of life. Years ago I paid a woman to care for my dog, Murphy. She would focus her attention on my fat retriever so I could focus on my addictions. She would drive Murphy to the vet and groomer, indulge her with treats and tummy rubs, and take her home when I stayed out all night. That woman likely spent more time loving my dog than I did. And for that I will forever bear the shame of my neglect.

Now I spend my afternoons visiting four-legged shut-ins whose owners are overscheduled and otherwise engaged. No one is happier to see you than a dog that needs to pee. I get more unconditional love in 30 minutes than most people do in a lifetime. My charges and I walk and play and cuddle. I give them super-sized helpings of snacks. I tell them they are kind and smart and important. And I make my amends to Murphy with each whisker I rub.

Along the way to my appointments, I am out in the world with other service providers. I am enlisted in the army of delivery people, maintenance men, housekeepers, nannies and cleaning professionals of all types. I watch burly men heave newly upholstered antique settees into 10,000 square foot mansions. I make friends with people dedicated to vacuuming air ducts and waxing woodwork and tuck pointing crumbling mortar joints. They are my brothers and sisters in solidarity—those of us who make life seamless for the rich and famous.

In my former life where outsourcing was the norm, I never knew who was in charge—never had sight of the complete picture: Who had the dog? The checkbook? My pants?

In my using days, I was never really present. Now—thanks to sobriety and poverty—I am able to fully participate in my own life. I have no Alfreds or Lurches or Rosie the Robots coming to my rescue. I'm my own clean-up crew. Fortunately, I have no nagging concern that the Rosarios and Mr. Frenches of the world will be without work because of my quasi-independence. I know there will always be those who require a little more help than the rest of us. In fact, I'm banking on it.

To be totally honest, I still, from time to time, employ the services of a gardener to assist in the maintenance of my yard. Old habits are hard to break. I consider it my contribution to Michigan's labor market.

My help's name is Michelle. She is a very curvy 20-something who weeds my garden scantily clad in a deliciously revealing bikini.

At only $10 an hour, I consider her quite the bargain.

TLL

There

I love going to recovery meetings. It has taken me nine years to admit, but I really do love them. Somewhere during the process of spiritual rebooting, my brain has switched from, "If I have to go to one more of those meetings I'm going to explode," to "If I don't get to one of those meetings right now I'm going to explode." Recovery is sneaky that way.

If I can quiet my mind long enough, I hear the most amazing stories. Many of them are just like my own—I just don't always recognize them because they're hiding somewhere in the waiting room of my mind reading an old *People* magazine with Freddie Prinze, Jr., on the cover.

The sad fact is other people tell my story better than me. It's like reading for the role of me in a movie about my life, and later finding out they gave the part to Meryl Streep. Apparently, she nailed the accent.

For those not familiar with 12-step meetings, they are pretty simple. Here in Michigan, we have mostly "table" meetings, meaning a group of folks sit clustered in a circle and share their thoughts and experiences on one of the twelve steps of recovery. Sometimes we read approved literature, sometimes we just wing it. All of the dialogue is extemporaneous, from the heart, brutally honest, and for the most part, filled with hope.

I have grown to know and love many of my fellow addicts. Truth be told, I seek out certain people because I am buoyed by their message. I avoid some others at all cost. I'm sure people do the same with me. It's only human nature that I sometimes get bored with the same people sharing the same stuff. You can watch only so many reruns, even of your favorite show. My sponsor once told me that if I liked everyone in the program, I wasn't going to enough meetings.

So it's a particular treat to have a new person at a table, be it a newcomer attending their first meeting or a visitor—perhaps someone in town on business. They are like celebrities making a cameo appearance, like Nathan Lane on "Modern Family." Their particular story is new and I am genuinely interested in hearing their message.

"Hi, I'm Bob, an alcoholic from Boston," is all I need to hear to get goose bumps on the back of my neck and sit a little straighter in my chair. It's Pavlovian. Maybe within his share, Bob from Boston will offer us the key to utopian sobriety. And so I sit in silent anticipation of his words—his experience, strength and hope.

Recently, I had such an experience. My face, known for telegraphing my every emotion, lit up as a stylish, unfamiliar young man—a complete stranger—took the seat next to mine at one of my regular 12-step meetings. Fresh meat, I thought, in the most spiritual of ways.

His name was William, and while he did not hail from an exotic locale like Boston or Buffalo, he was in the area visiting from Romulus, Michigan, a vast 22 miles away. To the delight of the table, William was a good talker. He requested we focus our discussion on the 8th step of recovery. Step eight requires that we make a list of all the people we have harmed through the selfishness of our addiction, and become willing to make amends to them. To laypeople, it sets the groundwork needed to apologize for being a lifelong asshole.

William said he was having a difficult go of it with number eight, and spoke at length about the fits and starts he had encountered to date. He was getting tied up in semantics and the need to be perfect—aka procrastination. William was a lovely man, well-groomed, well-spoken and impeccably mannered. His tone suggested heartfelt earnestness. Soon I was caught in William's journey, and his journey became mine.

William told us his sponsor had suggested he break from the noise and chaos of the daily churn to focus on his eighth-step list. A weekend get-a-way, the sponsor nudged, might be just the ticket to help with William's focus. Many of us in early sobriety possess very short (look, there's a chicken) attention spans. Guiding William out of his apartment and out of the nonsense in his head were the first steps to achieving eighth-step enlightenment.

Taking his sponsor's direction, William decided to drive to Michigan's Upper Peninsula. There, he would attempt to connect with his higher power, commune with nature, and find his spiritual center—all that touchy/feely guck we addicts call "recovery." In these unsullied surroundings, William, like Thoreau, would reflect, contemplate and come up with a fucking list.

For those of you unfamiliar with Michigan's northern peninsula—what we fondly call the "U.P."—let me offer a brief description. Actually, Michiganders are almost incapable of discussing the geography of our state without using our hands as physical references—thus being known as the "mitten" or "hand-puppet" state. The U.P. comprises one-third of the state's total landmass, yet only three-percent of Michigan's residents. The folks residing north of the Mackinac Bridge call themselves "Yoopers"—a kind of Sarah Palin of the lower 48.

These hardy souls enjoy 12 or more months of winter, have one interstate highway and teach "Overthrowing the Government" in elementary school. They can also walk to Wisconsin, for what it's worth. The United States Congress forced Michigan to adopt the U.P. and return Toledo to the Buckeyes as our price of statehood. While it sounds like blackmail, I think the government did whatever it wanted back in 1837—much like today. And, if you've ever been to the U.P., we mitten people more than won that deal. I'd take Copper Harbor, Hiawatha National Forest, and Tahquamenon

Falls any day over the home of Jamie Farr and the Mud Hens.

U.P.-ers are not a type-A breed. They don't have access to the iCloud, they don't speed date and they don't drive very fast. In fact, they don't drive anywhere. They have no destination. Driving to them is the noun, the verb and the preposition. They don't go anywhere, probably because there is no place of any relevance to go. At least down here in the lower two-thirds when we say we're going for a drive, we actually end up somewhere—a coffee shop, a friend's condo, a bar, jail. We go somewhere. Our goal is to get *there*. U.P.-ers simply don't see a need for *there*, and so begins our friend William's story.

Did You Remember the List?

For four full days William searched the topography of Michigan's U.P. for the perfect site to create a list of those he's wronged in order to repair the wreckage of his past. He drove from campground to waterfall to forest to sand dune in search of the ideal destination— the Canaan of recovery—to make contact with God. He sought an area with the best possible reception to ask God the question that's consumed man from birth, "Can you hear me now?"

However, in his attempt to get from beach A to campground B to observation deck C, William found himself stuck in a "U.P. traffic jam"—one Yooper going 17-miles-per-hour in a 1923 flat-bed truck with three hound dogs riding shotgun. The local appeared to be Jed Clampett—pre-bubbling crude. Jed and his pals were out for a casual drive, collecting historical artifacts along the way—a dented hub cap, a rusted license plate, a limited-edition Batman Returns Slurpee cup, three-fourths of a Queen-size box spring. Maybe he was more Fred Sanford than Pa Clampett, but we understood William's imagery.

At that point, William became unglued. He was on a spiritual journey to Serenity Island, but his luggage was still in Crazy Town, USA. As we all know, you can take the addict out of a nuthouse, but you can't take the nut out of the addict. Remove us from the bustling city, high-stress job, badgering wife, and barking dog and inside we're still a radio set at the wrong frequency and stuck on maximum volume.

I could live in a solitary underground bunker in Greenland and still find something to complain about. I'm like a five-year-old sitting in the back seat on a very long car trip yelling about my brother, "He's looking at me!"

My good friend Phil has developed a theory he calls the "Three Asshole Rule." He maintains that as you go about your day, you may run into one asshole (a driver who cuts you off at an intersection) or even a second asshole (the man who grabs the last peanut doughnut at 7-Eleven). But Phil says by the time you come upon the third asshole—likely an innocent person who's harmed you in no visible way—you, my friend, are the asshole.

Such was the case with William. He became a victim to his own inner asshole. We all have one. It floats somewhere between our inner child and our inner ear—usually punching inner peace in the neck.

"I wanted the old man to drive faster," William admitted, somewhat ashamed, somewhat surprised. "I wanted him to get the fuck out of my way."

William gestured with his hands, like a child might describe soldiers marching in rank.

"The sooner he moved ahead, the sooner I could, too. I wanted to get *there*."

As addicts, we're always trying to get there. Maybe that's true of the human race in general—not being an official member, I can't say for sure. I don't know the mass appeal of *there*, but for us, the grass (no pun intended) is definitely greener just up ahead.

There is a better restaurant, a closer parking space, a more satisfying relationship, a beefier paycheck, a better life. If we could just get there, all of our problems would be solved. Things would finally be good...*there*.

William's *there* was that perfect spot on earth where God would whisper the names of 12 or 43 people in his ear; the names he, in turn, would write down copiously in a spiral-bound notebook, and upon returning from his spiritual sojourn, proudly present to his sponsor, thus receiving an eighth-step star on his forehead.

Rarely do things work that smoothly. At least not for me. And never, ever have I found my spiritual salvation in the passing lane. The location of William's perfect place doesn't likely exist somewhere on the road ahead. I doubt he can locate it with MapQuest or a fancy GPS. He has to find it within.

I'll Be Right There

When I graduated from college, all I wanted was a condo with a cleaning lady, a convertible Corvette and an unlimited source of cocaine. In time, I checked those items off my wish list and added a host of enviable new collectibles: A mini-mansion—check. A wealthy husband—check. Vacations to private islands—check. A job that paid more money than I had ever dreamed and far more than I was worth—check, check.

In the vernacular of William, I got there. I got to the perfect spot—the land of milk and honey. I got all the things I ever wanted—I won the quality-of-life lottery. But *there* handed me a few surprises—some gifts I didn't request, such as alcoholism, cardiovascular problems, self-loathing and suicidal ideation. I got to the space William so desperately sought just up ahead, but for some reason there looked exactly the same. There wasn't what I wanted, either. In fact *there*, and its desperate seeing of, got me to places I never sought—rehab, mainly, the heart doctor, divorce court, unemployment.

I hazard to guess that William and I aren't the first people to realize that *there* often looks no different than here. The world is filled with poignant stories about people who, after achieving some superhuman goal—pro athlete, business tycoon, celebrity chef—chucked it all because the brass ring was too tight.

Wealth, or the absence of it, was not my lesson, nor was it William's. Spiritual awakening is not about career regrets or greed or the worship of false idols. I think God's lesson is about mindfulness—living in the here and now—and not in that mythical patch of imagined perfection lying somewhere west of I-75 Exit #386.

Living in the moment isn't always pleasant. It can be uncomfortable, like Bikram yoga. It forces you to face your fears, feel your feelings and become what addicts hate most—a grown up. God gave me a lot of "flight" but not a lot of "fight." I'd rather escape—physically or more often emotionally—than face my feelings. Feeling is probably the most feared activity on the planet. It ranks right up there with public speaking and being audited by the IRS. Why that is, I have no idea. I've asked and asked and asked, "Why do we run from our feelings?" Carl Jung says it has something to do with being eaten by a sabre-tooth tiger. I don't understand the Swiss.

Call Me When You Get There

William's story galvanizes the age-old proverb: No matter where we go, we are always there. Like the tortoise with his house on his back. When we find paradise on the road up ahead, we're still in the car. We can't outrun ourselves.

Here's what I tell myself: I'll never get *there*, because by the time I'm there, there has become here. I'm exactly where I am. And, according to my higher power, I'm always exactly where God wants me to be.

I'm Melting

In 1939 four desperate strangers, motivated by fear and emptiness, joined forces en route to a promised land. There, they believed, their wishes would be granted. They would each obtain the one missing element that would make them complete, thereby creating a perfect life. Like our friend William, it lay on the road just ahead.

And it would have worked out perfectly had it not been for that damn witch, her flying monkeys and that dorky professor with his Donald Trump hair.

But that is not the point (albeit an interesting thought to ponder later). The point is we are all wearing ruby slippers. We each have all the heart and intellect and bravery we'll ever need. Everything we want is already baked into us—ready-to-serve like Stouffer's lasagna. We are perfect right where we are.

A lot of people talk about the God-shaped hole inside of them. They spend years—some of them entire lifetimes—trying in every conceivable way to fill that hole. They might look in a shot glass, the neighbor's pants, a money clip or the corner office. Yet the only thing I've found that can fill the God-shaped hole inside me is—ironically enough—God. Unfortunately, I could not have picked God out of a police lineup for a very long time.

47

I was running, like Forrest Gump. To something? Away from something? Who knows? In the final analysis, I found I was searching for the peace and love and grace of God. Never did it occur to me that everything—the entire Kingdom of God— resided quietly inside me. I needed only be still and know.

My sponsor says, among a million other annoying phrases, "You are always okay." Whether it be this day, this hour, this minute or this finite second. Like I said, it's very annoying, but true. Some days that's the best I have to go on; being okay from second to second. But she's right; I always am (always have been and always will be) okay.

My good friend Betty puts it another way: "Bloom where you're planted."

I think I'll enjoy the dirt.

TLL

Take a Lesbian to Lunch

Now that my inner lesbian has awakened—something that happens to many gays in their teens and early twenties—I'm feeling the fury and sadness that someone my age doesn't easily have the energy to muster. At 52 I fear I'm too old to examine the social conscience of our great nation and its huddled masses. As an alcoholic in recovery, I don't know what to do with my feelings half the time anyway—adding choler to the mix might make my head explode.

I've never been much of an advocate, unless we're defending the sanctity of the afternoon nap. I'm not the kind to march around in circles carrying a handmade sign decorated with rainbow-colored poster paint. Unlike my hero Anne Lamott, I've never been cuffed and stuffed in the back of a patrol car, sat-in, picketed or boycotted in protest of anything. I vote conservative. I drive a Ford. Hell, I've even eaten at Chick-Fil-A and find its offerings quite tasty. But with everything going on in the world today, I feel compelled to do something. My gay brothers and sisters are being killed, beaten, denied and marginalized in ways that would have you thinking we were witches living in 17th Century Salem.

Therefore, I'm moving into action. It might not be the correct action, but at least I'm moving. It's time to launch operation "Take a Lesbian to Lunch (TLL)"—a plan that's been rolling around in my head for some 30 years.

It's based on a premise that's neither original nor unique: You can't hate me once you know me.

Now that I love me, I believe everyone else should, too.

Here's the beauty of TLL: there's no campaigning or fund raising, no robo-calls, telethons or membership drives of any kind. There are no buttons, T-shirts, doorbells, clipboards or complex bureaucracy. Like AA, there are no leaders, only trusted servants. The last thing we need is a special task force appointed by the president to improve gay relations.

TLL is aimed at eliminating fear-based ignorance—one misguided homophobe at a time. Unfortunately, much of what "Middle America" believes about gays is formed by sensational media coverage—outrageous behavior gladly provided by those on the rainbow fringe. A six-foot-five man (or woman) wearing only a thong and a purple Mohawk while rollerblading in a poorly organized parade is not the image I want people to have when they think of me. Continuing the stereotype that gays are unstable, counter-culture freaks does nothing to promote equality or normalcy, nor does it accurately represent the gay population.

Getting to Know You

I believe that TLL can tear down the wall between straights and gays though individual, face-to-face experiences. And what better experience is there than the social convention of breaking bread? Within the time it takes to eat a personal pan pizza, these two groups can begin knitting a peaceful coexistence, much like the practice of glasnost that ended the Cold War.

Every segment of the population is encouraged to participate in TLL. Like the Girl Scouts recommend, you are never too young or too old to make a new friend. Take the example of my best friend's mother, Grazyna. At 92, she eagerly accepted an invitation to meet her granddaughter's gay roommate, Stephen, a flamboyant flight attendant from Miami. Over pierogies and diet Cokes, Grazyna took an immediate shine to Stephen, so much so that she pegged him as the perfect future husband for her granddaughter. On the way home from lunch, she sadly remarked, "It's too bad he's a lesbian."

"Take a Lesbian to Lunch" is an overarching strategy to bring people together. The plan itself is very flexible and not to be taken literally. "Take" doesn't requiring hoisting a gay on your shoulder like a discount Persian rug; "lesbian" means any member of the LGBT community and "lunch" is not necessarily a noon-time meal. These are just general guidelines—much like Federal tax laws.

The first step is finding your LGBT—lesbian, gay, bi-sexual or transgender—dining companion. If you think, as did the aforementioned best friend, that these letters have anything to do with a bacon, lettuce and tomato sandwich, you will need to do a lot of pre-work before your first engagement.

Some folks in the LGBT community are easier to spot than others. A good place to start is a gay bar or café—predictable yet efficient—or some type of pet activity like dog park or animal adoption center. Gays also like events that require costumes—masquerade balls or "Sound of Music" sing-alongs. Other likely venues include your local hardware store or a Liza Minnelli/Cher/Bette Midler concert.

These suggestions are based on long-held stereotypes. While it may surprise you, not all gays attend Chaz Bono rallies or shop at Bergdorf's semi-annual warehouse sale. My partner Sharon, for example, would not signal anyone's gadar. She blends right in with the heterosexual women buying eye makeup at the Aveda counter. Our friends Gail and Vivian are leading lady beautiful. Both wore stunning white dresses on the day of their wedding, a photo of which could have appeared on the cover of Bride's magazine. My friend Rick, who neither lisps nor wears mascara, has classic Robert Redford looks—rugged, handsome and strappingly straight. Come to think of it, much of my gay posse resembles the cast of a 1990s hospital drama. It's many of my straight friends who look suspect.

Once you find your gay, the next step is to plan your lunch. As I mentioned, feel free to vary the meal. It can be breakfast, brunch or a late-night snack. Try coffee. Or a fruity cocktail. Gays like their fluids.

Do not consider "take" to be a verb, like "take out the rubbish." You physically don't have push your gay in a stroller or carry them in the basket of your bicycle. Nor are you required to pay for your companion's meal. Please note, however, that lesbians are known to be extremely frugal. In the event you do make the choice to "Go Dutch," do not be surprised if your lesbian limits your dining options to locations offering "buy one get one free" meals—yours being the "buy" and hers being the "free." I suspect, however, that in the blink of an eye you'll be so enamored with your new LGBT BFF, paying their tab will be the least you'll want to do. You'll likely end up buying them a luxury SUV or inviting them to live with you, or perhaps knitting them and their Pomeranian matching Christmas sweaters.

I'm Cancer, What's Your Sign

Okay, you've got your gay, you're seated in a coffee shop, what comes next? This moment might feel awkward. Relax, this is completely natural. Start slowly. Pretend that you're meeting a visitor from a foreign country, but don't shout or gesture excessively. You don't want to dive into a heavy conversation about the economic benefits of compound interest or how to freeze sperm. Make it light. Make it pleasant. Talk about the weather. Hobbies. Hobbits. Pets. People love to talk about their pets. Go back to the time when you first met

53

your college roommate. Reenact that exchange: Where do you live? What's you major? Do we have any of the same classes? Do you have any pot?

Once you've cleared the social underbrush, you are likely beginning to form an opinion of your gay, something like, "Wow, we like the same authors," or, "She has five fingers on each hand just like I do," or, "He really loves his Peekapoo." Now you can begin wading into the deeper end of the pool, personal stuff like careers, parents and kids. You are now transitioning into experiencing your gay as an individual—vulnerable, wounded, capable of loving and being loved.

Your gay is no longer just a garden-variety LGBT, they are Martha or Chad, Amy or Richard. Her parents threw her out of the house at age 15. He was bullied in gym class. She prayed to God to make her straight. He was outted and discharged from the military. She contracted AIDS. He was president of his college fraternity. She has breast cancer. Her daughter was killed by a drunk driver. His partner committed suicide.

To fully experience the beauty of the moment, try to open yourself up in return. Walk into the moment. Share the times you felt judged or weak or less than. Was there a time you didn't fit in? Was there a time you wished you were someone else? Were you ever bullied? Were you ever the bully?

Force yourself to look past the exterior packaging. Do you still feel better than? Different than? Are you still standing in judgment? Are you beginning to feel a human connection?

Hopefully by now, you are staring at the shattered remains of your pre-conceived notions scattered on the restaurant floor. If so, congratulations! You have done what few people are willing to do: open themselves to change. If not, I encourage you to try again. You may have just gotten a bad gay. I admit that the LGBT community has its share of rotten apples—we're not exempt from being assholes like the general population. I apologize for Rosie O'Donnell and Perez Hilton.

We're Not All Sally Field

Unfortunately, I have found that the "Take a Lesbian to Lunch" movement is not guaranteed to make you like me. Despite all my positive attributes—I rescue animals, I'm back to flossing daily, I donate generously to our city's high school marching band—you may find I'm not your cup of tea. I can live with that. I can accept that you think I gossip too much or laugh too loudly or even that I'm a bit slothful. If your negative opinion of me is based solely on your experience with me, I'm willing to let bygones be bygones. But please don't base your assessment of me solely on who I sleep with. I doubt you want me judging you on the same criteria. If that that were case, who'd be pals with Rihanna?

Wishful Thinking

After years of intellectually perfecting my TLL strategy, I believe the plan is ready to go viral. It is

55

simple, based on the purest of intentions and it appeals to the good in all of us. Who among us wants to be a "hater?" Who among us doesn't want to give peace a chance? Seriously, do you want to be the last gay basher on the planet? The last person who still smokes cigarettes or believes a woman's place is in the kitchen? The last person who eats lard? Of course you don't.

However, I've been told by a few friends in the gay community that my master plan may be built on faulty logic. Apparently, in some circles, the more someone gets to know you, the more they may actually dislike you.

"It is the wishful thinking of a child," a fellow LGBTer said to me upon learning the specifics of my plan. "You're naive. If it was all so easy, my partner and I would have been eating Thanksgiving dinner with my family for the last 12 years instead of at Wing Ling Gardens."

Unfortunately, my sad friend may be right. Just look at world politics. Some guys in the Middle East hate the U.S. no matter how many church socials or poker games we invite them to. Do you really think Bill O'Reilly or Ann Coulter are being invited back on *The View* any time soon? Fred Phelps still has followers. When the hate is that visceral and engrained, it might take more than a potluck dinner to bring us all together.

Maybe TLL is just a fantasy. My own father threatened to disown me when he discovered that my high school sweetheart was a girl, and he and I had had a lifetime of lunches together. My 83-year old neighbor, the one who calls me her "surrogate daughter," doesn't believe in equal rights for homosexuals.

"You don't need any specials rights," she screeched after we errantly wandered onto the topic, rich with land mines.

"I'm not asking for special rights," I yell back, my voice a full two octaves higher than normal. "I just want the same rights everyone else has."

In that moment I felt connected to everyone, everywhere who's ever been told, "You're not welcome here."

No Change, Some Hope

When news broke that the Senate voted to lift the military's 17-year ban on openly gay and lesbian service members, that same loving neighbor made a beeline to my doorstep.

"Where will they sleep?" she questioned me breathlessly.

"Where will who sleep?" I asked.

"The gays."

"Where do they sleep now?"

"But they're going to want to have sex."

"Doesn't everybody want to have sex?"

No matter what, it always comes down to sex. Why do straight people think we gays are constantly trying to get in their pants? Seriously, is it paranoia or wishful thinking? I've had many men in my day make unwanted sexual advances toward me. I didn't find it any more or less offensive when lesbians did it. None of the people I've ever dated in the gay community have been insatiably horny, I'm disappointed to report. I sometimes wish lesbians were half the sex-crazed maniacs straight people make us out to be. Just because we have sex with members of the same sex doesn't imply that's all we do. We find time to hold down jobs, have hobbies, walk our pets, pay taxes, volunteer and parent our kids. We're not just hiding in the bushes and waiting to abduct your daughters for an *L Word* viewing marathon.

Sometimes I think the only bright spot in the world is Tel Aviv. While everyone else in the region wants to make gays into falafels, Israel recognizes same-sex couples, has numerous anti-discrimination laws on the books and even allows gay couples to adopt children. If that's not enough, television's first same-sex dance pairing was seen on Israel's *Dancing With the Stars*. I guess it takes a persecuted people to demonstrate real compassion while offering top-notch entertainment.

I don't know where all the hate comes from, nor do I think my brilliant plan for straights to break bread with the LGBT community will quell the acts of violence and injustice perpetrated on us. I'm not telling everyone they have to hop on the gay bandwagon. I'm not even asking politely. I'm merely suggesting that no one go out of his or her way to kill us or otherwise make our lives impossible.

There is No "G" in Charlotte

When are people going to see that being gay is a very small part of who I am? It does not define me, it does not explain me, nor does it allow anyone to put me in a small box based on their own limited awareness. I would think by now my extreme "Charlotte-ness" overshadows my gayness, anyway. Being a lesbian is the least of anyone's concerns. Humanity is more likely to be offended by my politics, the smell of my aging Ford Escape, or the fact I let my dogs and cats eat off my fork. And that's just for starters.

Unlike former New Jersey Governor Jim McGreevey, I don't refer to myself as a "gay American," any more than I consider myself a German American or a Michigander or even a Spartan or Wolverine. I don't distinguish myself using terms like "educated" or "conservative" or "among the ranks of the unemployed." My program of recovery instructs me to relate to others, not compare. When how you look at life changes, what you see changes as well.

This is really all you need to know about me: I am a child of God, same as everyone else.

God made me the way I am, and no, I do not think He was having an off day. The only choice I have when it comes to my sexual orientation is whether to hate myself or love myself. If I choose the former, I may go the path of former Rutger's student Tyler Clementi and all the homosexuals who take their own lives, defeated by shame and guilt. If I choose to love myself, I can be of service to my fellow man—be he gay, straight, purple, a deer hunter, a liberal or even Tom Ryan. Hey, if I'm asking him not to judge me, I have to be willing to do the same for him. And for the people who practice Sharia law, have abortions, don't have abortions, are Mormon or Muslim, and want the power to decide how much trans fat I can have in my Big Mac.

For the Record

This is all I want: A little house filled with pets, someone to share my life, the freedom to praise the God of my understanding, the ability to pursue limitless abundance, true friends and an honest butcher.

Oh yeah, and that "All men are created equal" thing that was so popular with Thomas Jefferson and his pals.

Dude, we've been waiting like 240 years.

TLL

Live Long and Prosper

The Irish are a toasting people. Not the transitive verb, as in exposing sliced bread to radiant heat, but rather the noun—the thousand year old custom of waxing eloquently while hoisting a frothy mug in revelry. I've been to enough Irish wakes and weddings to have heard my share of pithy patter about absent friends and beautiful women.

Irish toast the living, the dead, the newly married, babies, bachelors, holidays, potatoes, luck, fornicating and drinking. They are especially fond of toasting the drink. As an alcoholic, I think the practice of keeping the night alive and the bar open by simply inventing a few clever verses is brilliant. I might still be drinking today if I could find a word to rhyme with cirrhosis.

Another common theme among Irish toasters is longevity. The notion of an insanely long life appeals to the Irish, which is ironic, because an eternity of mowing my roof and eating boiled entrails makes we want to die immediately. But to the Irish, life without end is the Holy Grail.

"May I see you grey and combing your grandchildren's hair."

"We drink to your coffin. May it be built from the wood of a hundred year old oak tree that I shall plant tomorrow."

"May the good Lord take a liking to you...but not too soon!"

"May you die in bed at 95, shot by a jealous spouse."

I wonder if such toasts have run their course. In 1900, "ripe old age" was 46. I'm sure "'Til death do us part" seemed like a good idea to Leif Eriksson. But today? How can humans expect to mate for life when our life spans have almost doubled? I think we need to change our mating expectations, starting with, "After age 37 everything's negotiable."

If This Condition Exists for More Than Four Hours, Please See a Doctor

Another popular Irish toast, "May the doctor never earn a pound out of you," is also out of touch in today's society. We seek affordable, quality health care like miners panning for gold—and with equally dismal prospects.

My parents, for example, lived to be doctored—probed and tested like white mice in a sea of medical red tape. They were like Ponce de León searching for the elusive fountain of penicillin. Maybe they had watched too many episodes of *Marcus Welby, M.D.*, and *Medical Center.*

Their calendar was marked not with birthdays or piano recitals, business meetings or heartworm reminders. Instead, each checkerboard square contained information regarding a doctor appointment. My mother claimed to have sinusitis, arthritis, gingivitis, diverticulitis, melanoma, cardiomyopathy, high and low blood pressure, bad good cholesterol, bad bad cholesterol and colon polyps. And it didn't stop there. Mother convinced me at an early age I came from a long line of neurotic women.

"It's okay," she reassured me when I complained of anxiety at age seven. "We all have bad nerves."

To help me bear that pathologic cross, mom started giving me Valium in junior high. It substantially reduced my performance anxiety on exams, oral presentations and at band concerts. Who knew "Mother's Little Helper" worked for daughters as well?

Heal Thyself

It should come as no surprise that I have both an obsession and repulsion for modern medicine. I am the daughter of my parents—afflicted with the doctor bug and drawn to latex gloves like a rat to bacteria-infected cheese. I am also leery of anyone wearing a white lab coat. I want to stop the cycle of external validation through lollipops and tongue depressors.

My doctor fascination began early in life. I was born, the legend goes, with a hole in my heart the size of a Kennedy silver half-dollar. Given I was born in 1963 and that particular coin wasn't minted until the next year, I wouldn't put a lot of stock in the veracity of that legend.

Anyway, medical science was purportedly perplexed with my situation—this was, of course, long before Dr. Jarvik's miraculous mechanical invention or the baby with the baboon's heart. The cure in my case was to do nothing, which became a kind of motto for me in later life. My condition called for regular visits to hospitals and diagnosticians. I was the only one I knew frequently released from class to be strapped to an examination table and connected to a variety of machines with wires, buckles and a substance appearing to be Vaseline. The exams always concluded with me back in my polyester school clothes sitting in my pediatrician's office with Dr. Kleiburn, 100 pounds overweight, smoking a Lucky Strike and telling my mother, "She's fine."

As a girl, I loved the attention I got from being sick—milking even the most minor affliction for days on end. Instead of playing with phony pots and pans, I played with ace bandages, wrapping myself silly. I think the first badge I received in Girl Scouts was for organizing the troop's first aid kit.

My doctor obsession culminated during my active addiction. I shopped at various clinics and pharmacies to obtain medications for fabricated conditions—pills for mysterious maladies that doctors were all too happy to oblige. Today I am terrified of all narcotics, and am constantly having to remind doctors, "No means no!"

Let's Get Physical

I made the mistake of getting a physical today. I was actually guilted into it. Have you watched television lately? The AMA and big pharmaceuticals have me believing that at age 52, I'm a ticking time bomb. I'm like Paul Reiser just waiting for an alien to burst out of my navel.

Every commercial tells me I suck. I should sleep better, look better, have more energy, burp less, have more sex, have a much better memory and (what was that last thing?) oh yes, ask my doctor if (fill in name of popular new drug) is right for me. I don't know about the rest of the country, but after hearing the side effects of most new prescription medications, I really doubt they are right for anyone. If, by law, 50 seconds of a one-minute drug commercial is dedicated to disclosing the possibility of bloody stools, vomit, heart failure, amnesia, nerve and muscle damage, change in skin pigmentation, loss of smell, blindness, black urine, uncontrollable itching, hallucinations, violent psychotic behavior, fecal incontinence, suicide and sudden death, I think I'll pass.

There are actually mediations categorized as sledgehammer drugs because the risk of death is about equal to any benefit derived. Come on—is it really worth dying to get a few more winks or a little more nookie? Whatever happened to, "Take two aspirin and call me in the morning?" I guess the same thing that happened to house calls, bedside manner and affordable health care.

I recently learned that pharmaceutical companies target certain types of programming to run their drug ads. I would prefer not hearing about prostate problems, erectile dysfunction and acid reflux during my few hours of televised entertainment. Maybe I should just cancel cable.

My favorite drug ad is for Zoloft, featuring a sad little misshapen blob that looks as if it's been drawn by a five-year old with a purple crayon. Apparently, Zoloft makes you bounce, which I think should be the goal of all antidepressants. Perhaps the best time to run this ad is during daytime soaps. Seriously, if after 12,000 episodes you're still willing to dedicate five hours each week to the continuing drama of *General Hospital*, you should be heavily medicated.

The Doctor Will See You Now

Upon entering my physician's waiting room for my annual exam, I immediately eyed something amiss. It was not the usual geriatric crowd reading back issues of *Reader's Digest* and examining the contents of their used Kleenex. Sitting, instead, on the heavily brocaded Queen Anne chairs was a sharp collection of nattily dressed men and women hard at work on iPads, toting stylish leather bags, and remarkably not showing the symptoms of any persistent illness. No wet coughs, no vomiting, no visible signs of blood loss or open sores. These people appeared quite well, as the afflicted go. Too well, I spied. Joking with one another. Exchanging information.

Generously proffering small plastic bags filled with branded pens, Post-it notes and nasal inhalers.

These were no patients, I deduced, these were pharmaceutical reps. And they were smuggling in everything from acne cream and analgesics to Red Wings tickets and boxes of Krispy Kremes. Here was an entire team of FDA-approved dope dealers and I sat defenseless among them. Just one complimentary pill from these voodoo priests and I'm back in a Minnesota rehab center without the benefit of mouthwash and using round-tipped scissors to make sock puppets.

It's no wonder doctors go through prescription pads faster than golf balls. Pharmaceutical companies push drugs like Girl Scout's hawk cookies. Instead of Tagalongs and Do-Si-Dos it's Prozac and Cialis. While they can both provide a temporary sense of euphoria, I understand they can also kill your sex life.

She Gives Me Fever

Unlike most folks I know, I actually enjoy my yearly physical. My internist is a young Polynesian woman with an exotic beauty that quickens my pulse and drives my temperature up a degree or two. I enjoy flirting with her in my usual clumsy and embarrassing way, trying to be witty and charming and not at all sickly.

That can be a problem, because I sometimes am—sick, that is. And having a childish crush makes it so much more difficult to say words like "discharge" and "boil." How can I possibly show my hemorrhoids to a woman I

67

dream of one day conquering on the white beaches of Bali?

Today's exam was actually quick and mostly unremarkable. Blood work good. Blood pressure good. Reflexes good. Healthcare insurance good. But just like my parents, I was placed on the appointment merry-go-round—directed to make three follow-up appointments. I was first sent to a urologist to find out why I'm retaining liquid. In this economy, I think my bladder feels the need to hold on to every asset I have.

Next was a mammogram. You know, if the people at Microsoft and Apple are so smart, why can't they develop a breast-screening app for the laptop and smart phone? Instead of having to go to the hospital, put a gown on backward and tape metal BBs to my nipples, why can't I just sit down at my computer, take off my bra, run the mouse around my breasts and call it a day? Isn't universal breast-cancer prevention at least as important as playing football with John Madden or launching *Angry Birds*? I'm just asking for a modern alternative to vice grips. Screw the pink ribbon; this could be a real contribution to defeating cancer.

The third follow up was for an echocardiogram. Apparently my heart still sounds like a Cuban percussion section 52 years after being born with a hole in it. What I find amusing is that somewhere along age 17, I remember being told that it had completely healed. I guess I can say without hyperbole, you really can't mend a broken heart.

And in the spirit of full disclosure, I was also diagnosed with bursitis. Good God, how humiliating. I believed bursitis to be a condition of blue-haired women who rocked on front porches with the ability to predict precipitation and cold weather systems. Mine is in the left shoulder and makes it hard for me to scrub my back and cast a fishing rod. Good thing I'm right shouldered.

Out of Order

I read recently that medical science is prolonging human life well past the body's natural ability to function. In short, we're living past our expiration dates, outlasting our warranties. Who needs a hip replacement or new heart valve if we're supposed to be dead, anyway? It's like replacing the floor mats on a Jeep with 950,000 miles.

Perhaps God did not intend us to be nonagenarians and beyond. According to the Bible, after Methuselah, who lived a record-setting 969 years, God ratcheted back man's life span due to our various and collective wickedness. I doubt God has proclaimed us any more virtuous, especially with Michael Vick in our ranks. His existence alone should have shaved another 18 months off our life expectancies.

Maybe if the Obama administration has its way, there'll be a new governmental ruling on how long we're allowed to live. Maybe that's the secret bullet in reducing healthcare costs.

I think there was a *Star Trek* episode about a colony of people who all lived in perfect health until age 70. Then they voluntarily turned themselves in to die. What a deal! Living every day free from even the most remote sniffle, but always knowing when your lease is up. I would definitely max out my credit cards right before my 70th birthday.

My 84 year old neighbor regularly corresponds with one of her sorority sisters who lives in Connecticut. Corresponds the old fashioned way—manila envelopes, multiple stamps, do not bend, takes five to seven business days to deliver. Several times a month, they send enormous packages back and forth to each other containing newspaper and magazine clippings of recent events, interesting activities, and the comings and goings of celebrated people. Truth be told, the packages contain horror stories clipped from the headlines revealing some new court ruling, hideous crime, social trend or global disaster. Both ladies are staunch conservative Republicans and are at no loss for material. With Hillary Clinton, murder rates, healthcare reform, teen pregnancies, stem cell research, mainstream media and network programming, they've got a landfill of bad news travelling the 1,000 miles between states, but at least they're helping keep the U.S. Postal Service afloat.

To punctuate her dismay at the articles, Mrs. Connecticut attaches Post-it notes to every clipping. Her mini editorials read: "Liar!" "They're all crooks!" "Rat Bastard!" "I'd like to see him burn in Hell!" and "Slut."

My favorite comment is, "We're doomed!" In fact, we've nicknamed the Connecticut sister, "Doomed."

When my neighbor and I coffee-klatch over "Doomed's" latest installment, the only thing that cheers her up is the pleasure of believing she'll die soon.

"At least I won't be around when 9/11 happens again, Oprah becomes president, China invades the U.S., or a million other things happen," she announces with glee. "I'll be long gone and you'll have to deal with the mess!"

Her laughter is both wicked and genuine. I can tell I'll be hearing it from beyond her grave.

"Wait a second," I interject. "Isn't it me who's supposed to be bragging that I'll be outliving you?"

"With the economy, Social Security and property values in the tank, weak national security, pink slime hamburgers and all those teenage vampires running around, I'm ready to go right now."

She's not joking.

"And," she concludes, "Every damn part of me is wearing out. I'm falling apart piece by piece."

At that moment, I conceded to her logic. The thought of living another thirty, forty, or even fifty years doesn't seem like the prize it once was—especially with my achy shoulder, mis-timed heart, and pissy bladder. I guess longevity is not all it's cracked up to be.

Someone alert the Irish.

TLL

The Banquet

I'm not a fan of parties—not even when I was drinking. The bigger the bash, the less likely you'll find me there. I'm not a big small talker, I don't move well in crowds, and I don't like standing—especially in one place—too long. Who can balance a tiny plate, a napkin, and a glass of juice while trying to hold up your end of a conversation? You need to be an octopus—forget cutting your pork tenderloin or passing the artichoke dip. I always leave feeling hungry, crabby, and wondering why I bothered getting out of my pajama pants. Feel free to add "doesn't socialize well" to my list of character defects.

I've used just about every excuse to decline party invitations—even those thrown in my honor. I once bailed out of Easter dinner with my parents, telling my dad that my dog had blood in his urine. How Tobi's pee affected my ability to eat HoneyBaked Ham was a mystery even to me, but it worked perfectly to get me off the hook.

Most people disagree when I tell them about my feasti-phobia.

"Shut up," someone will tell me. "You're the most outgoing person I know."

Having an annoyingly loud laugh isn't at all the same as being gregarious. Sure, I can be the life of the party, but that's if it's a party of three. Put me in a retirement party or wedding reception of 300 and I'm looking for the exit. My favorite hangout is inside my house, waving silently as the party bus drives by.

I've been told I miss out on a lot of good stuff being the way I am. I'm fine with that.

God, on the other hand, loves a good bash. The Bible is filled with parables about banquets and feasts—feast being the popular term for "house party" back in Jesus' time. I'm told "feast" is an allegory referring to the kingdom of God. Being invited to a feast is God's invitation for us to climb upon His throne and receive the power of the Holy Spirit. And maybe a Jell-O shot.

It's what we humans *do* with God's party invite that is generally the theme of these biblical tales.

The Wedding Feast

Luke, Matthew and Thomas all wrote versions of Jesus' parable of the great wedding banquet. The circumstances and details differ between them, but the essence is the same. I offer below an amalgam of the three, with apologies to my brothers in Christ.

A wealthy king embarked upon hosting a banquet—a wedding feast—to which a number of wealthy, busy and important people were invited. Apparently, because no one owned a clock back then, the king sent his servants at the appointed time to notify the guests the great

73

banquet was to begin. Not only did the king's friends not own watches, they had very bad manners. One by one, the guests began backing out, saying they had other, more pressing business—ancient stuff like buying yokes of oxen and maiming poor people.

When the servants reported back to the king that all of his friends had dissed him, the king sent his minions back out. "Offer them further enticements to come— fatter cattle and gift bags by Givenchy. That ought to do it," he said.

The obedient servants revisited the invited guests, who were not only steadfast in not attending the king's party, but were growing angry at what they perceived as royal harassment. So angry, in fact, that a few of them murdered the king's servants on the spot—hence the term, "Don't kill the messenger."

The remaining non-murdered servants returned again to the king and said, "Dude, back down. This party is so not happening."

But the party was going forward, with or without these snooty guests. The king gave his servants new instructions: "Bring in the poor, the crippled, the blind and the lame." The faithful servants did as they were told, even returning with tax collectors, prostitutes and thieves. The king and his newfound degenerate peeps rocked it into the wee hours, and then went to White Castle for sliders.

As parables go, I thought this one pretty obvious. I was quite proud to report back to Diane—my spiritual

Sherpa and mental health professional—that I had in no time decoded God's intended message.

"I get it," I said with great enthusiasm. "This story is about how people like me don't make time for God. I would have been one of the guests who stayed home and manufactured a dumb excuse like 24-hour leprosy to avoid the banquet."

It is—in the end—the persecuted and disadvantaged that show up to the King's banquet, even though they're called last and view themselves as unworthy. These are the people God wants at the party all along. They need redemption, they need salvation, they deserve a break today.

I told Diane we all need God's invitation—rich, poor, virtuous and misguided. We all get the call, but few of us choose to accept God's grace. And, like the king, our job is to share the word, especially to those people we judge harshly, those we shun, misunderstand and pretend not to notice. We must scour our hearts to find those people, for they need our compassion the most.

Finished with my peculiar brand of biblical interpretation, I folded my arms in satisfaction. I awaited my gold star. Instead, Diane shrugged and rolled her eyes, revealing once again my limited understanding of most things in life—the Bible in particular.

The parable, Diane told me to the contrary, was not a trite story about right and wrong, as I often perceive life to be. It wasn't about bad people making bad choices,

75

nor did it suggest that some of us are more deserving of God's love than others.

"The parable challenges us not to witness the differences in people," she said, "the rich and poor; the just and unjust. It challenges us to see the similarities among us. Each of us is every person in the story—we are the king, the lame, the wealthy, the murderer, the married, the obedient and the abandoned.

"We all accept God's grace and we all turn from it. We honor, corrupt, seek revenge and offer refuge. We reject ourselves and we reject God. We are forgotten and lost and then found. We must acknowledge the many parts of ourselves and accept the totality of who we are. That is, after all, exactly how God made us."

I didn't like her interpretation at all. I was willing to accept that I didn't make time for God. I was even willing to admit my selfishness, my harsh judgment of people, and the fact I should be more compassionate to the people who need it most. But I did not see myself in every person in the story, nor did I want to.

Setting the Table

Many years ago, I attended a seminar by John Bradshaw, bestselling author and expert on toxic shame and emotional healing. He lectured for most of the day on those topics, then asked the audience to participate in an exercise that haunts me still. He asked us to imagine in great detail an elaborate banquet—a private feast where each of us is the only invited guest. In my mind I created something quite opulent—a freestanding gazebo with walls made of glass. There were fragrant flower arrangements with gilded decorations, ornate columns festooned in garland, and a stately tabled draped in beautiful linen, set with fine china, crystal, and silver.

Bradshaw instructed us to conjure up all of the likeable parts of ourselves we wished to invite—the best of our best. I started making my mental list of good Charlottes. I invited the fresh little girl—the one who sang solos at the elementary school Christmas pageants. I welcomed the honor student and high school class president. I invited the upwardly mobile 20-something with the taut ass and quick wit. I invited the MBA graduate and business executive. Of course I invited the elegant woman with fine jewelry and beautiful gowns. I invited the dutiful daughter who indulged her parents. I invited all the women who prospered and flourished in circles beyond my childhood imagination. I was quite pleased with my assembled selves, a formidable collection of educated, accomplished and respectable women. I reveled in the "mes" I had succeeded in becoming.

We were interrupted by our speaker with a new development. At each of our private banquets, unwelcome guests began arriving. These party crashers, said Bradshaw, were the disowned parts of ourselves that caused us shame. These were the Charlottes I hid from others and even denied myself. Immediately I saw their dirty faces pressed against the glass. They were cold and hungry, dressed in rags. They were frightened and alone. They were the shadow selves I kept locked away. I felt their shame and abandonment. I was sickened by my own cruelty.

Bradshaw directed us to invite them in. I looked around at my alienated selves. The teenager who stole pot from her sister. The co-ed who abused her partner. The young woman who neglected her family. The arrogant woman with no time for God or for those less fortunate. The drug addict. The alcoholic. The lesbian. I was surrounded by lost souls sick with secrets.

I hated these versions of me—the cheat, the bully, the coward, the miscreant. I could not let them in. I could not give them permission to be so very bad.

And so I left the banquette and its half empty seats—untouched place settings for my unwanted selves.

He's Such a Heal

Exercises like the banquet invite us to heal by offering compassion to our shame-bound selves. Rather than keeping them in exile, Bradshaw says, we must accept these fractured selves as a necessary part of us—as lovable as the part that rescues stray cats and takes soup to elderly neighbors. He believes these selves also serve an important purpose.

Not the Guy from Beauty and the Beast

I am a big fan of Robert Benson, author of *Between the Dreaming and the Coming True*. In his book, Benson writes about the true nature of who we are. He believes that while still in our mother's womb, God whispers to each of us the word—in my case, "Charlotte." I am, he says, the only person who will ever know what God said to me.

"God whispered the word (Charlotte) to me, and no one else. If I do not hear that word, no one will. If I hear it and fail to act upon it, no one will. In the world to come I shall not be asked, 'Why were you not Moses?' I shall be asked, 'Why were you not (Charlotte)?'

"The will of the One who sent us is to be the one who was sent."

Forgiven

My sponsor thinks it's time for me to go on a recovery retreat. I can't think of anything I'd like to do less. The theme of this particular retreat is "Expect Miracles." I haven't expected a miracle since discovering the self-cleaning litter box. Spending 40 hours at the Skyline Conference Center in Almont, Michigan—wherever the hell that is—sounds only slightly worse than a Molly Ringwald movie marathon. After achieving some amount of continuous sobriety, I thought I'd be free from monotonous activities like weekend retreats and doing God's will. Guess I was wrong.

To make things worse, participants at the retreat will be challenged to examine their character defects. "Defect" is the politically correct term we recovery people use for our shitty behavior patterns. "Defect" sounds almost innocuous—like a misfiring sprinkler head or third nipple or the inability to properly pronounce the word "nuclear." But we alcoholics know there is nothing innocent about our defects. To us, defects are moral shortcomings that cause us to behave immaturely and wreak havoc on the planet. Our defects are no mere "door dings" on the Cadillac of life, they are the cracks from which our alcoholism flows.

I've spent a lot of time with my sponsor and therapist working on my character defects. I've asked for God's help in removing the most glaring of them—obvious wrongdoings like selfishness, dishonesty, sloth, anger, intolerance and fear. For me, just about everything boils down to fear. Fear I'm not enough. Fear I'll die alone. Fear of the unknown. Fear of running out of pet food.

While I'm far from being "fixed," I believe I'm making progress. I no longer have road rage or spend countless hours under the covers fretting over things I can't control. I put my mother, my finances and my furnace in that category. Since our recovery motto is, "Progress not perfection," I believe I'm moving along the improvement continuum at a comfortable pace. I guess that's why my sponsor is suggesting the retreat. She rarely wants me to be comfortable. It's only in churn that we make real progress, she says. I inform her that taking a crash course in self-examination is more than just discomfort—it's downright irritating. Maybe it's my sloth, intolerance and fear talking.

Two other women in our group—girls with much less sober time than me—have already registered for the big event. They jumped at the chance for a weekend of defect purging. Both of these women also have young children and annoying husbands. They aren't fooling anyone. They would have signed up for bull-riding lessons or a weekend in the county jail just to get away from their families.

The Darker Side of Me

I don't want to think about my shortcomings. I don't want to admit that after many years of sobriety, I can still act badly and very often do. I don't want to be reminded that character defects are no different for me than drugs or booze—I can only ask God for a 24-hour reprieve. I can only try to be the person my dog thinks I am, one day at a time.

My true desire is for the wreckage of my past to lie quietly buried, or at least on the other side of the glass. I don't want to be confronted with the imperfect me that remains very flawed. I want to believe that because I live a different life today I am immune from my own destructive behavior. I want to believe I am no longer bad. But, as my therapist says, a house divided against itself will not stand.

Because most of my secrets have been published for all to see, I want to close the book on the old Charlotte. I want today to mark the time I begin walking on water, healing the sick and baking all of those delicious loaves of bread.

But that's apparently not my job. My job is not to be Jesus, but instead, Charlotte. And that means making peace with the woman who will continue to deceive and betray and abuse. Who is dishonest and irresponsible and selfish beyond measure. While I want to take a sharp knife and cut her out of me, I must, Bradshaw instructs, warm and comfort her. Nurture and welcome her. Offer her a seat at my most holy feast.

If God made me to be exactly the way I am, then He intended me to have these very imperfect parts. Disowning them would be defacing His handiwork. Maybe the lesson of being a human includes shattering the illusion of perfection.

Maybe one day I'll see the good in me. The whole of me. For now, I wrestle with the many faces of Charlotte and my God-crafted shadow self.

Benson writes that God's universal symphony requires my word. Without it, he says, God's song won't be complete.

Sometimes, I have a hard time believing I am the Charlotte God whispered into song.

Sometimes, I have a hard time remembering my word.

TLL

Death Becomes Him

It was recently brought to my attention that the devil has been defeated.

I'm embarrassed to report: I missed that newsflash completely.

I guess I've been spending too much time watching *Downton Abbey*.

As with all things of great importance, this information was delivered to me by my best friend via a shirt-tail relative of hers. Without doubt, she is always right, and I implicitly believe her in all matters, especially pertaining to our spiritual selves. However, this devil thing seemed way too big a news story to have been overlooked—by me and everyone I know. Satan slain: That's a combination moon landing, Berlin Wall busting, Princess Di passing, levy flooding, presidential impeaching-sized historic moment. It's the proverbial shot heard 'round the world. I must really like that Lady Mary.

In comparison to the newsworthiness of today's events, isn't Satan's destruction worthy of an interview with Geraldo Rivera? How about a segment on Rachel Maddow or even a Joyce Meyer podcast? Shouldn't his undoing generate at least as much coverage as the execution of Saddam Hussein or the dog with the world's longest tongue? You'd think this would be the kind of thing the Christian Television Network lives for. I can just imagine the membership opportunities.

I double checked today's top stories. The Exorcist is celebrating 25 years on film. Carmina the cat was installed as the new head feline at the Washington National Cathedral. Pope Francis chucked his chauffeured limousine for the Buenos Aires subway.

Lucifer—zip.

What the hell happened?

The Witch is Dead

I assert that the devil's decimation is enormous news, even to the liberal media. In fact, I suggest we put aside our usual political and theological squabbles to toast, with sparkling cider, this auspicious occasion. Maybe we can assign a federal holiday to this landmark. Surely if we can celebrate "Metric System Day" and host an annual remembrance for Punxsutawney Phil, we can acknowledge the undoing of the underworld.

What is the appropriate celebration for this type of event? Ticker-tape parade? National day of prayer? As I recall, the Munchkins sang a little tune when Dorothy's house smashed the Wicked Witch of the East. The Ewoks celebrated their victory over the Empire with a galactic-wide furry luau on Endor. We can surely do something appropriate to celebrate hell freezing over?

Someone please call the Pope or Martha Stewart for advice.

Mephistopheles is Not My Name

While Satan's obliteration is apparent good news for the human race, I'm afraid his departure will wreak havoc with our popular lexicon. How will we express feelings of rage without making reference to hell or Satan or other aspects of the nether region? The devil may have been vanquished in the battle of good versus not so good, but his absence may keep us tongue-tied for all eternity. Can anything really replace these seemingly irreplaceable phrases?

- "Your dinner tasted like hell."
- "She put me through hell."
- "Shut the hell up."
- "It was hotter than hell in July."
- "Your mother drives like a bat out of hell."
- "Hells bells!"
- "Lenny's a little devil."
- "She damn near killed me."
- "I'm very horny."

What do angry drivers do when we can't even tell the asshole ahead of us to, "Go to hell?" When Flip Wilson's sassy catch phrase, "The devil made me do it" has no context? Does this mark the end of the Sun Devils and Blue Devils and New Jersey Devils and Devil Rays? Or wave a sad goodbye to devil's food cake, Halloween and the night that precedes it? What about the tiny unincorporated community of Hell, Michigan? Who—I ask—will now ride on my other shoulder—the one opposite the little guy with a halo? Should I put up a help wanted sign, "Accepting applications: No pitch fork required?"

Hell: For Sale or Lease

The devil's defeat seems to have great global significance, at least as much as revealing the next cast of *Dancing with the Stars*, yet I see nothing that suggests people are addressing the many issues raised by his demise. First and foremost, what happened to everyone in hell? Where have they all gone? We're worried about the president closing Gitmo because we don't know what to do with the detainees, but with hell's gates open, every bad guy from Jack the Ripper to Richard Nixon is free as a bird.

How about the real estate in hell? Is it now available? It might be an option to consider for retirees when Florida goes in the tank. And what about all that roasting and smoldering and burning? Maybe it's the devil who's responsible for global warming. Can we redirect some of that warm air to Michigan, where no one I know can afford their home heating bills? And did anyone tell AC/DC that their popular highway is closed?

Uncivil Disobedience

We earthlings may not like the idea of hell, however, nothing in the history of mankind has done more to improve our overall behavior. Hell is the ultimate "Wait until your father gets home." That sentence scared me straight (not "straight" straight, but "straighten up and fly right" straight) every time my mom used it.

What will I personally do without a hell? Will it completely change my behavior? I'd be lying if I said no, which is one of the many things I'd do if indeed hell is in foreclosure.

Won't people go fucking insane—knocking over liquor stores and shooting each other and having massive orgies? Perhaps 21st century earth—post devil—will make Sodom and Gomorrah look like Disneyland.

I think that's exactly why Satan's defeat has been covered up—it's a conspiracy of biblical proportions. The existence of hell is too strong a behavior modifier to abandon publicly. Without the fear of the prince of darkness lurking about, I don't think any of us are pure enough to be civilized. Face it, without hell, I can't be trusted on my own.

Good vs. Evil, Take 1

Once my indignation over being out of the loop on the whole dead devil thing subsided, I went to the Internet. I wanted to know what was really going on. If the devil had indeed been eradicated as my friend suggested, I didn't want to be the only one thinking he was just living in South Beach or at the Jersey shore.

To believe the devil is dead, I guess you first had to believe he was alive. I know many people who believe

Satan is a very real enemy—the unrelenting adversary of God and humanity. They blame the devil for creating chaos, suffering and all the evil in the world.

Others—agnostics and atheists—believe religion is just a mystical set of handcuffs to keep us all in line. If God is merely a tale concocted by cavemen afraid of lightning and death and wooly mammoths, hell is just a natural extension of the story. Hell is man's insurance policy that we keep our hands to ourselves and leave our pants on. If you're not afraid of the IRS or a night or two in jail, you may feel differently about spending eternity on a Weber grill. Whatever your opinion, you have to admit it's been an effective deterrent—whether you believe the devil is a bad dude in a red suit, the remnant of an ancient superstition or just a metaphor representing evil. Without whatever the devil is, we might be royally screwed.

Ashes to Ashes

To my great surprise, I learned that Christians actually do believe the devil has been defeated. Since I claim to be one of them—a Christian, that is—I suppose I should have known. That said, it's not as simple as it sounds. Scripture takes us down two seemingly contradictory roads. One has us believing the devil lost the war over death and sin through Jesus' victory at the cross. The other tells us Satan is still at work.

That's pretty hard to swallow. How can he be both defeated and among us? It seems an oxymoron—like jobless recovery or soft rock or sanitary landfill.

According to the apostle Matthew, Christ accomplished a decisive victory over the power of the devil through His death and resurrection. But, and here's the baffling part, Matthew also says the devil's still on the loose, "Prowling around like a lion looking for someone to devour." Devouring is not at all comforting.

Revelations claims the devil will try to win a final victory over Christ, His church and His people on the last day. The good news is (and this is a spoiler alert) the devil and all his ungodly forces will be defeated forever, "Cast into the lake of burning sulfur, to suffer their ultimate defeat and torment day and night forever." And thus will begin God's uninterrupted eternal reign of love—cue the flying cherubs, chorus of angels and release the doves.

We are now, says Matt, in the mopping up phase—a time between the victory accomplished on the battlefield and the end of the war. We are, say biblical scholars, awaiting Christ's return and our day of final liberation. We are waiting for the holy fat lady to sing.

Defeat, the Sequel

Maybe man's triumph over evil is much like my own victory over addiction. I claimed victory on March 23, 2004 when I finally put down the booze and dope. But the celebration was short lived—24-hours, to be exact. I get only a daily reprieve from my disease based on my spiritual condition. There is no definitive win—no ultimate cage fight; no Super Bowl of sobriety. Like Matt said, I'm just in the mopping up phase. I was a very messy drunk.

People say the devil is in the details. I say he's in my ego—whispering shit that can only lead to disaster. My ego tempts me in the same way Satan tempted Christ. It tells me: "I can drink with impunity," or "I have power over alcohol," or "All the kingdoms in the world are mine if I just smoke that rock."

Today I know those are just lies. One day at a time I surrender to my higher power, and I'm okay. I heard a friend in the program once say, "Religion is for people afraid of hell; spirituality is for people who've already been there."

Thank you, but once was enough for me.

TLL

I Do... Not

My mother and dad loved each other, and hated each other, for more than 50 years. Most folks I've known have never had the privilege or the perseverance to achieve such a feat. My parents were married in the early '50s—my mother at age 28 and my dad a few scandalous years younger. The ceremony was held late in August, on a day described to me as "hotter than hell" and without the relief of modern air conditioning. Their vows were exchanged at 11:00 a.m. during a full Catholic mass. The men wore cutaways and striped trousers, the women carried calla lilies and smelling salts, lest a member of the bridal party succumb to the extreme conditions. The reception immediately followed in the basement of a Bavarian café popular with my grandparents and their people. Legend has it the cake melted into pools of curdled frosting; the handsome topper washed away and was never seen again. Perhaps foreshadowing the life that lay ahead.

Many of my mother's relatives traveled from Germany for the occasion. They were apparently horrified by the weather, and drew a number of conclusions about America and Americans based on the heat. Germany, or should I say West Germany, as it was known before the wall fell, was described by my grandmother as always cool, extremely civilized and generally superior to the U.S. in most ways. Everything in my grandmother's hometown of Mulheim was pleasant, clean and correct. And cooked in pork fat.

The marriage produced two daughters—my sister in 1959, and me four and a half years later. The union survived living with my mother's parents, which was typical of the times, a short stint in a starter home on the east side of Detroit, and a move to Riverview, where I was raised. It also survived my father's alcoholism and my mother's crush on little yellow pills.

I cannot—with only one exception—remember any intimacy between my mother and dad, be it emotional, physical, or spiritual. I did interrupt them having sex once in all the years I lived at home, which is an embarrassing sum considering I moved home four separate times after graduating college. Between my mom and dad, there was no canoodling on the couch, no holding hands at the movies, or lingering kisses goodnight. Their connection was a mystery—unless you counted the fights, which were epic and frequent.

My parents yelled. And swore. And said terribly mean and ugly things to each other. Things people are never meant to say and that can never be taken back. The fights were either ignited by my dad's drinking or my mother's complaining. They seemed to last forever.

My sister and I would hide behind the second-floor banister listening to the battle. She was less concerned about the outcome and more interested in the cause. Had we done something wrong? Did someone scratch the car? Were our grades bad? Did someone take the last can of Coke?

I Mean it This Time

My fears were immobilizing. I listened to every harsh word, paralyzed, and braced for the final, "I'm leaving," or "We're through." Then what would happen, I questioned? Where would we go? What would we do? How quickly would we cease to be a family?

Back then, in the very middle-class Detroit suburb of Riverview circa 1970, divorce was rarely mentioned and then only in a whisper. A very small handful of schoolmates had fractured families, and those kids were frowned upon, pitied even. The decade of the '70s was all about staying together for the sake of the kids, regardless how that togetherness would shape (or damage) them in future years. I was treated to human behavior at its worst, repeated and repeated like a very bad episode of *All in the Family*.

As I grew older, I became less attached to my parent's arguments. My mom would come to me on a regular schedule—every six weeks or so—proclaiming she was divorcing my dad. She would pack a bag and retreat to her mother's house—with or without us kids in tow. She sought pampering and justice and deliciously crisp potato pancakes. No one was hurt by her temporary abandonment; my father seemed to enjoy his time alone immensely. My mother's absence was punishment to no one. Except maybe my grandmother.

When I was old enough, I copied my mother's pattern and fled to my grandma's to escape the warring. I was welcomed with open arms, strudel, and *Wheel of Fortune*. It was Oma who taught me the permanence of love in what otherwise appeared to be a very conditional family.

After I was married, my mother began seeking refuge at my home. It became my job to entertain her for days on end—fancy restaurants and shopping sprees and breakfasts in bed. She believed it was also my daughterly duty to badmouth my dad, take her side in every argument, and agree that her life was overwhelmingly hard. My mother never had a hard day in her life—except for the days her soap operas were pre-empted by the Watergate hearings. She visited her pharmacist more than usual in the spring of 1972.

Just Keep Going

That is how I learned about relationships. Fight. Run. Return. Repeat. Pretend like nothing happened. Don't talk. Don't change. Just keep the cycle going.

Why did they stay together? Who knows? Appearance? Apathy? Maybe it was a Catholic thing or a shame thing (today I know they are the same). Maybe divorcing was a version of personal failure—something my dad would never admit to. I'm sure money played into it. Going back into the workforce after 50 years was certainly not on my mother's bucket list.

Maybe to them, there was simply no alternative. Just like every Michigander who complains about the long winters and allergy season, perhaps my parents believed marriage was just a part of life's suffering. Maybe happiness never entered into the equation. After all, wasn't marriage historically about building strategic alliances and procreating farm hands? Weren't engagements brokered by third parties to unite wealth and class? Wasn't it just an easy way for the groom's dad to score some gold bars and a handsome new ox?

Adult Education

In the schoolhouse of interpersonal relationships, Mom and Dad were my only teachers. Oma's husband died when I was three or four. So did my dad's mother. My sister had her husband thrown in jail. Other than what I saw on TV, I had no understanding of how people behaved in loving relationships. My Oma became the only teacher of love—but that was love between a grandparent and a child. Not the kind of love Prince Charming had for Cinderella, or Ken had for Barbie, or Mike Brady had for Carol.

As a likely result of what I was and was not taught as a child (in addition to that whole drug addiction thing) I've had a string of unsuccessful and messy relationships. I, too, have communicated through yelling or ignoring. I have used violence. I've fled, detached, pretended, and obsessed. Most of all, I've stayed. Stayed in a very dysfunctional relationship for six years and a questionable marriage for twelve. I'm now in a partnership that's coming up on ten years. It's definitely had its ups and downs, as I suspect most relationships do. I would certainly not hold myself up as a poster child for ideal mates. At best I can say I'm improving with age, like an alcohol-free wine.

I've been told by a number of folks in recovery that all alcoholics are bad at relationships. Like most character defects associated with addiction, I don't believe mismanaging relationships is exclusive to the population known as drunks—in recovery or out. I just don't believe that coupling—or whatever you want to call it—comes naturally. To anyone. Relationship savants are few and far between. If someone tells you they're the perfect catch, go ask their other half. Chances are that perfect catch is a work in progress, much like a home in constant need of repair. Just when you think it's safe to host your in-laws for the weekend, the roof caves in and you find mold in the crawl space.

The Right to Fight, Legally

People who study our species—I guess they're called anthropologists—say humans are a monogamous breed given to pair bonding for life. I'm not sure I agree. Despite what I think, we humans—Americans in particular—are sure making a big fuss about the right to do so. Legally, that is. Apparently, the brass ring of the pair bond is marriage. It's a sanctioned union—like the Ultimate Fighting Championship—that comes validated by the government, God (according to those who speak for God), and public opinion. If two people are married, by gosh, that seems to be all that matters. Just don't ask too many personal questions.

Here's what it takes to get a marriage license in the state of Michigan: Photo ID and $20. If both parties are at least 18 years old, no other terms must be met. Not even a blood test. Oh, I forgot. One of the parties must be male, the other female.

Up until recently, that was pretty much the requirement for all states. If you can pass the one man, one woman test, have a valid driver's license, and can afford the price of two beers and two hot dogs at a Detroit Tigers game, you're in. You and your betrothed can be married in a church and can avail yourselves of certain rights not offered to non-married people.

None of this makes sense to me. First, no one can convince me they know God's mind. Why does He care where people are married or by whom, for that matter? Second, I don't believe certain people should get certain rights others aren't entitled to have. Everyone should be treated equally. Call me an idealist. Or an American.

According to CNN, some members of some religious groups are changing their position on the whole marriage thing. These people now claim that God is, in fact, okay with same-sex unions. Apparently, the one man, one woman requirement has timed out. I'd like to ask these people what other issues God is purportedly flip-flopping on. I'm already eating meat on Friday and I've officially given up on Latin. One more transgression and I'm officially Presbyterian.

Certain states are now legalizing same-sex marriage—37 as of this writing. I'm often reminded by seemingly well-intended people that many of these same states have legalized marijuana. I'm not quite sure of the connection, but I certainly understand the connotation.

Quick, Before Someone Changes Their Mind

On March 24, 2014, a U.S. District Court found that Michigan's denial of marriage rights to same-sex couples was unconstitutional. Yes, for one progressive day in my home state, same-sex couples could legally marry. On that singular day, gays and lesbians—many who'd been in decades-long monogamous relationships—stood in near-freezing temperatures to exchange marriage vows that were finally recognized by judges, tax collectors and county clerks.

Then all hell broke loose.

The very next day an appellate court, thanks to State Attorney General Bill Schuette's emergency motion, stayed enforcement of the ruling. Former U.S. Attorney General Eric Holder stepped in, extending federal recognition to those 323 marriages performed on March 24, so that those families might receive federal benefits. Eight months later, Michigan's ban on same-sex marriage was upheld. While it came as a surprise to no one, it was a dark day nonetheless.

The ordeal has left a lot of people here feeling confused and angry, and disenchanted about marriage altogether. That's in addition to those already feeling queasy about the institution pre-March 24.

And the Right to Be Miserable

I saw a hilarious bumper sticker the other day: "Stop protecting homosexuals, legalize gay marriage." It made me think of my parents' marriage. I laugh at the thought that gays are fighting for the right to be as miserable as that one man and that one woman were for more than 50 years. I just don't see a life of long-term suffering the same badge of honor they did—legal or not.

I know all marriages aren't bad. As I mentioned, I was married for 12 years. A few of those years were the very best of my life. The irony of my marriage was that he and I should have remained just friends. Exchanging rings really fucked up our relationship.

When my ex-husband and I notified my parents we were divorcing, my dad thanked us for ruining his vacation. He and my mother were leaving a few days later on a trip to Hawaii to drink cocktails with tiny umbrellas and fight in a $500-a-night hotel room. After that news, Dad didn't talk to me for months. He also removed me as executor of their will and decided I was no longer the favorite offspring. Considering I had just paid for the Hawaiian vacation, I thought the consequences quite severe.

Iowa is for Lovers

Today my partner and I have a very good relationship. That's reason enough not to tamper with it. We have no legal right to marry in Michigan. I guess I could in Iowa, but seriously, who but a lesbian would travel on purpose to Iowa?

Anyway, she's not interested. Her parents split before she could ride a two-wheeler; she sees no glamour in the institution. For years, however, I desperately wanted to marry her and even proposed a few times. Perhaps it was to be considered more normal, perhaps so that I could finally get it right.

I've since learned two very important things: One: Never want in desperation. Two: Normal is overrated.

I don't need someone else confirming that Sharon loves me, or that I love her in return. We're not asking for anyone's permission. So I'm not eligible for her Social Security benefits or whatever. Anyone who thinks that fund won't go bust way before I turn 70 deserves to meet Bernie Madoff.

Does a marriage certificate guarantee we'll be together forever? That we'll be happy? That in 10 or 20 or 30 years she'll still look at me the same, that look that says, "I can't believe I'm in love with such a nut?"

There are no guarantees. Not in relationships, not in marriage, and certainly not in life. At the risk of getting my official lesbian membership card revoked, same-sex marriage is not my fight. But I do stand by the people whose fight it is. Especially when kids are involved. When marriage is the glue that makes a family—makes it legal for joint adoption and gives parental rights to both moms and dads—then I say legalize gay marriage on a federal level and stop the nonsense once and for all. Heterosexual couples do not have a monopoly on good parenting. Ask anyone born in the '60s. Or the Duggars.

For what it's worth, I believe a loving union is already blessed by God. He's not interested in the particulars of our genitalia. Nor does love require any human approval. Take it from someone who knows firsthand, love will not be denied.

Take My Wife, Please

To commemorate their 50th wedding anniversary, my parents renewed their marriage vows at a special mass held at their Catholic church. It was quite the big deal. All the relatives were invited, Dad wore pants with a metal zipper and Mom had her hair done high.

Someone, I don't remember who, bought them corsages. My ex-husband Peter offered to pin my dad's flower on. They huddled in the corner of the anteroom fiddling nervously while I did the same for my mother in a fellowship room down the hall. Ours was likely the same space where countless grooms took last breaths as single men prior to exchanging their own wedding vows. The irony was not lost.

That day found my mother in a particularly foul mood, even for her. Anything out of the ordinary had a tendency to set her off and this was certainly out of the ordinary. My father, deserved or not, was the target of her ire. Even after he stopped drinking and smoking, the poor bastard couldn't do a single thing right in her eyes. He might as well have stayed permanently pickled, considering her constant verbal tirade.

"Your father is a god-damned bastard," she said to me, not under her breath. "We won't make it through another year. I should have left him years ago. I don't know why we've stayed together this long."

I rolled my eyes and thought the same thing. Then I wondered why, here in the 21st century, pinning a stupid corsage remained such a difficult task.

Her rant continued—something about his driving, the parking lot, and maybe the way he buttered his toast. It really didn't matter. By then I had learned every fight with them was the same.

What I didn't know at the time, and what I learned later from Peter, was that he and my dad were having a very similar one-sided conversation.

"That woman is a pain in the ass," my father complained throughout the pinning ordeal. "Nothing's ever right, nothing's ever good enough. Bitch, bitch, bitch. Do you think she could be on time just this once? She'll be late for her own funeral. And she'll still be bitching from the grave."

Peter, officially the nicest guy on the planet, likely nodded in concurrence. He wasn't going to argue with my dad about anything, least of all his mother-in-law, whom he often referred to as "a piece of work."

So there it was. Fifty years of holy matrimony. Fifty years of wedded bliss. Fifty years of nagging and complaining, nit picking and back biting, hurling heinous remarks and the kind of terrible insults you wouldn't say to a serial killer. That was the institution of marriage, presented by my folks for five decades without commercial interruption.

After the last-minute details were attended to, the priest gave a signal for my parents to enter the church. They would lead a processional of elderly couples—each celebrating a major marriage milestone—the length of the church. My mother and father walked arm-in-arm down the center aisle, beaming like moony-eyed teenagers. If you didn't know any better, you would have actually thought they were in love.

At the altar they knelt on a padded bench, received a series of blessings from the priest, and—like 50 years earlier—exchanged the promise to love, honor, and obey.

Then they kissed.

It was like watching Neil Armstrong bounce around the surface of the moon but swearing it was actually taking place on some gigantic Hollywood sound stage directed by Stanley Kubrick. My eyes denied what they were seeing.

A minute later, they were returning down the aisle, my mother smiling demurely, my father nodding in recognition at the fellow parishioners. They owned the moment and were selling it.

When they reached their original mark—the place where their deception began—one turned left, one turned right. Dad was very much in earshot when my mother continued where she had left off.

"If he thinks for one minute I've got nothing better to do than cook for him every night while he sits in that chair..."

She didn't miss a beat.

My father, I later learned, was relieved the ordeal was over. He was about to eat a big plate of chicken parmesan—his favorite food in the world (along with chocolate ice cream, Almond Joy bars and ranch dressing)—at a reception he had arranged at a nice little Italian restaurant on the Detroit River.

Unlike the original celebration of their nuptials, there would be no sauerkraut, no Bavarian sausages, or herring of any sort. Apparently, he had learned something in the last 50 years. I was delighted we both had.

TLL

(Author's note: Please see reference pg. 252.)

Faceless

From the time I was very young, I was told technology would make my world a better place. Better, defined as more efficient, more carefree and definitely more fun. It was just a matter of time before Rosie, a sassy robotic maid, would assume all of my cumbersome chores, leaving me free to whirl around in my flying car to visit Mars and live under the ocean in a geodesic dome. While some of those predictions have come true—like babies conceived in test tubes, Wi-Fi and artificial cheese food—we have yet to develop self-cleaning clothes, intelligence pills or my personal favorite, the paperless society.

What we have invented, and what seems to be only growing in popularity, is an alternative method of communication. I didn't know the old ones were broken. Apparently it was all those hand-written letters, phone calls and face-to-face conversations that were crippling modern society. Today our preferred method of talking is not talking. Instead we e-mail, text, IM, tweet, post, poke and stream. We use a thick bandwidth of digital technology to keep from engaging in the most human of all human experiences. We no longer wish to speak.

Our race to be quicker yappers has all but ruined the art formerly known as verbal intercourse. We're becoming a culture devoid of social skills, incapable of greeting someone a simple, "Hello" without using our thumbs and a fully charged battery.

Yes, Virginia, this is a rant about the newest generational gap. It is my dad's version of, "Turn that racket down and get your hair out of your face."

What We Have Here is a Failure to Communicate

I don't have a smart phone, nor am I interested in wrapping myself in an impenetrable cone of technological silence. For those who do, the iPhone and other similar devices can help you achieve a life of voluntary solitary confinement.

Modern technology has devised the imaginary BFF, part servant, part life coach, part wet nurse. This iNanny always has time for you, loves your vacation videos, thinks your taste in music is impeccable and spends its life butt dialing from your ass. What carbon life form would track your favorite sports teams, organize your business expenses, remind you of your daughter's upcoming piano recital and serve as your BIC lighter at a Neil Diamond concert? In return you never have to buy it lunch, never have to listen to it bitch about its wife and never have to admit, "Yeah, you were right." You can drop it on the ground, send it virtual viruses and even swap it out regularly for a newer, sleeker model. It is incapable of forming a resentment. Try finding that in a person.

According to one gadget newsletter, apps of all types are being devised to avoid archaic face-to-face dialogue. One app was expressly designed for people with an Apple-induced sense of superiority and disinterest in conversing with mere mortals. It allows users to order and pay for their morning Starbucks without ever having to engage in barista banter, exchange currency or make eye contact of any type. Whatever happened to Mr. Coffee? Apparently he's developed Asperger's syndrome.

iQuit

As usual, I'm swimming against the digital tide. I still seek out opportunities for human interface—to try out new material, preach recovery and probe into strangers' lives for my general amusement. I can't imagine consolidating these exchanges into 140 characters or less. How else would you find the best price on cat litter or which neighbors' lives resemble the Jerry Springer show?

The answer to this seemingly rhetorical question? Most people don't give a shit. Those totally immersed in the technology of communication have already walked away from society in a disconcerting way. According to a University of Michigan study, today's students are less likely than their Baby Boomer counterparts to describe themselves as "soft-hearted" or to have "tender, concerned feelings" for others. The bottom line: Even as they become more electronically connected, young people are caring less about others. Real others, that is. Apparently, they still have compassion for vampires and zombies.

That Generation Text, with their endless and real-time connectedness, would rather spend their time with the digital undead is troubling. Researchers caution us to brace for a real decline in basic traits like self-sacrifice and charity. That's unfortunate. Even Lieutenant Commander Data eventually got an emotion chip installed. Perhaps we're growing into a culture more Borg-like than human.

This generation of texters was raised on violent video games and 24-hour cable television. They were then cast off to college with a laptop, cell phone and a few hundred passwords. Born in the '80s, they are the young pioneers of the digital age with thousands of virtual friends, but no intimate bonds. They might claim to have a BFF, but down deep it might just be a pixelated FWB. As one researcher put it, "Technology has connected them, but in a very shallow way. You don't really have an emotional connection with someone on Facebook."

A few months ago, my partner Sharon and I were seated at our favorite Mexican restaurant, eating our burritos at the counter and staring blankly at the 1940-built movie theatre across the street. Into view came a stream of identical looking pre-teens walking in a kind of penguin shuffle, eyes to the ground and all performing the exact same motion with their flailing thumbs—something you might see in a petting zoo or perhaps psycho thriller. Then Sharon said the funniest line I'd heard her say in years.

"I bet they're all texting each other."

I bet they were.

Mona Lisa, Are You Texting?

Kids have their own da Vinci code going. They're shutting out their uninformed parents just as their parents did when they were young. Rather than using the words of Hunter Thompson, Bob Dylan, or Lennon and McCarthy as generational subterfuge, this new culture has created its own private language. That's all well and good for teens trying to outfox nosy moms and dads. It's another thing when your much younger girlfriend sends you emoticons that can't be deciphered even with the aid of a Cracker Jack decoder ring. How am I supposed to know that ~~:-(means she's getting rained on or :-X means she's sending me a big, wet kiss or that *<l:-) (Santa) +<:-) (the Pope) and := (a beaver) just walked into the bar?

Text messaging has become this generation's pig Latin. AT&T now offers a tutorial that decodes acronyms meant to keep parents in the dark about their kid's conversations. This includes POS ("parent over shoulder"), PRW ("parents are watching") and KPC ("keeping parents clueless"). I thought the last meant

109

you wanted a bucket of chicken but were a bad speller. Most of my friends are parents: I don't think it takes the mind of a master criminal to keep them completely oblivious to their offspring's goings on.

One pal told of his recent comeuppance at the hands of his daughter. Driving a squad of tweeners home from the mall, he noticed an unnatural silence in his SUV. Looking in the rear-view mirror, he saw his daughter texting furiously. Remembering his own formal upbringing, he scolded his daughter for her bad manners, explaining how rude it was to text while her friends sat idly by.

His daughter responded flatly, "But, Dad, we're texting each other. We don't want you to hear what we're saying."

I guess etiquette isn't the top concern for kids who every day pass through metal detectors on their way to homeroom or need batteries for spelling bees.

Fast and Furious

Expediency is the end game for this generation. God forbid a moment pass between the time a thought is formed and it appears as a post in a virtual diary. In my program of recovery, I'm encouraged to wait as long as possible between impulse and action. On the contrary, there is an almost frantic need for this new generation to share every life experience the second it unfolds. Why is it I need to see a photo of your dinner plate? Why are you required to "check in?" Perhaps they doubt that without immediate documentation an event doesn't really happen. As philosopher George Berkeley might say, "If a tree falls in the forest and I don't have my camera phone..."

Oh, yeah. What's a forest?

I Want Your Text

Technology is influencing our relationships in strange new ways. Are they better ways? Only time will tell. According to www.datingsitesreviews.com, one in five people have dated someone they met online—one in ten of us have admitted to sleeping with someone we met on Facebook. With one third of the world's population surfing the web, I guess it was bound to happen. I'm just glad I met my partner the old fashioned way: At a dog park.

Statistics show nearly half of us have sent illicit text messages to somebody other than our partners; while another 35 percent included explicit pictures of themselves. It's no wonder; the man who invented this social network craze began by comparing women to farm animals. He really didn't set the bar too high. Maybe it should be called something other than "face" book.

I'm not a proponent of such digital dalliance. Just look at the former mayor of Detroit. Kwame Kilpatrick allegedly exchanged some 14,000 text messages with his former chief of staff Christine Beatty, many describing in graphic detail an extramarital affair between the two.

No one should ever text the words, "My nigga! I love you, you know that."—if the intended receiver is not your current wife, despite how beautiful the sentiment may be. It's the 21st century version of lipstick on the collar that can't be washed away.

People are tagging all types of bad behavior to the digital world, warranted or not. A survey of 100 top firms finds that Generation Text often don't understand key aspects of office etiquette, use texting shorthand in resumes, and wear nose rings and flip-flops to work. These clueless employees use words like "dude" with superiors and have email addresses such as honeyhole69@hotmail.com. Perhaps this up-and-comer is looking for a job in the mayor's office.

Selective Retention

MIT professor and clinical psychologist Sherry Turkle is a self-proclaimed expert on cyber-scepticism— a term coined for people who distance themselves from reality through social media. Turkle's book, *Alone Together*, is a disturbing look at the way our hyper-connected world reduces our ability to sustain relationships and has slashed our (squirrel) attention spans. She contends that technology has captured us in an alternative reality that is a poor imitation of the real world. Turkle claims that the glue holding our society together is beginning to dissolve.

"Insecure in our relationships and anxious about intimacy, we look to technology for ways to be in relationships and protect ourselves from them at the same time."

While I'm no match for an MIT Ph.D., I caution the good doctor from Cambridge not to get too generationally superior about this latest craze. Technology did not invent bad behavior. People have always been insecure about relationships and anxious about intimacy. That's why Haagen-Dazs and flavored vodkas are so popular.

If you're my age, Ms. Turkle, you can wipe that ;o off your face. Our generation is fueling this fire—letting kids text in church and giving cell phones to seven-year-olds as birthday presents. We buy the game consoles and iPads. We use smart phones to babysit our kids and to keep them quiet in fancy restaurants. They are not interlopers; these devices have replaced Valium as mom's little helper. Seriously, who among us wouldn't like to have "The Talk" with our kids by simply sending them a text with a couple instructive links?

Like dope dealers, we're looking for ways to hook the newest generation of cyber babies. And why not; digital toys for the lunchbox set is a multi-billion dollar a year business. Just last fall, Firefly Mobile introduced the glowPhone for preschoolers; it has a small keypad with two speed-dial buttons—one for mommy and one for daddy. Please! What modern preschooler has a set of those?

As for etiquette, Ms. Manners, the arbiter of all things proper, ruled recently that e-mails needn't bog

113

themselves down with traditional salutations such as "Dear." The built-in heading and subject line are sufficient, she told a gentle reader. I can just imagine my grandmother having received such a memorandum from my 18 year old ass:

Heading: Cookies
Sent To: Oma
Reply To: Starving College Student
Delivery: Immediate.

I could have heard her foul German response all the way to East Lansing without the aid of a personal telecommunications device.

Even the Catholic Church has gone digital—sanctioning an iPhone app to encourage lapsed followers back to the faith. "Confession: A Roman Catholic app" is described as a "personalized examination of conscience for each user." What's next, on-the-go microwaveable communion wafers?

Here's a glimpse of my generation. We hid Mad magazines inside our text books. We ran ear plugs from our transistor radios to listen to afternoon Tigers' games during math class. As for talking during dinner, I learned to keep my mouth shut and eat. Funny how we remember things the way we want to, not necessarily the way they were.

Today's generation doesn't have a patent on shitty behavior. My dad told me I was selfish, sloppy, disrespectful and dimwitted, and I was born in 1963. I don't remember people applauding hippies for claiming free love, greasers and their hot-rod cars, or even preppies with all of their pink and green alligator sweaters. Here's another news flash: People were having meaningless hookups when the only technology out there was apple wine and when blackberries were saved for Sunday pies. Not everything is the fault of Steve Jobs or Bill Gates. Folks have always had the proclivity to be iNoxious, just as they are also wired to be kindhearted, generous and caregivers.

I don't fear the apocalyptic demise of our planet based on the sales of digital mini-pads any more than I worry about the Avian flu or why so many bed bugs are on the prowl.

I'm sure the kids will figure it out, just like we figured out cruise control and Adam Ant and Slurpee machines. I don't believe technology can suck the human out of human beings. At least it hasn't so far.

TLL

I've Been Jobbed

A Chrysler ad featuring hometown hero Eminem claims the city of Detroit has been to hell and back.

I, apparently, missed its triumphant return.

Everywhere people are talking about the state's economic recovery as if it's an undeniable truth like the proverbial duo, death and taxes. I don't see it. Factoring in part-time or "underemployed" workers, Michigan is still suffering double-digit unemployment. Any statistical decline in jobless claims is the result of discouraged job seekers permanently dropping out of the labor force. Private-sector jobs are not returning quite as quickly as reporters' claims, thanks to companies greedily grinding their much smaller workforces into Kibbles 'n Bits.

It has long been clear that economists and elected officials do not experience the world the way the rest of us do. This disconnect is especially pronounced when politicians can speak the words "jobless recovery" without cracking a smile.

What does all this mean to me?

I still can't find work.

With continued doom on my employment horizon, I've been looking for even the tiniest speck of light. I got it the other day when I heard a radio ad by a national home-improvement chain calling for temporary workers in preparation for its spring-selling season. Outstanding, I thought. I love spring, I love plants, and I love playing in Mother Nature's compost pile. This was a perfect opportunity—a God given coincident.

It was also a true spiritual awakening. How far I had come, I thanked God, from that arrogant egomaniac who wouldn't consider manual labor or a minimum wage job if her life depended on it, which it apparently now does. So before I could think any more about it and likely think myself out of it, I drove to our neighborhood's premier do-it-yourself superstore in hopes of claiming a coveted red apron and nametag reading, "Hi I'm Charlotte, I can help!"

Fill Out These Forms

I'm not sure what employment tests are required to pilot a trans-Atlantic aircraft or become a forest ranger, but I doubt the process could be any more grueling than applying for part-time work at this big-box store or its across-the-parking-lot rival.

Over the course of the last seven years, I conservatively estimate I've filled out 25,000 job applications. That said, nothing much surprises me in the world of job seeking. I've been asked the color of my skin, if I've been arrested, and whether I sleep with men or women. Given the state of my personal finances, I don't have the luxury of being cagey or offended.

But this process—for the job of loading 40 pound bags of topsoil into minivans—was more comprehensive than even my mortgage application. I wanted to sell petunias, for God's sake, not purchase weapons-grade plutonium. I didn't want to marry this Fortune 500 provider of affordable power tools. Did they really need to contact my third-grade teacher?

I Tested Negative

Not unlike a blind date, the Home Giant job application started with softball questions—did I have any relatives currently employed by the monolith, had I been convicted of a felony, would I consent to a background check, did I speak English.

Then began the real digging. They wanted my driver's license number. Perhaps they were simultaneously seeking out illegal aliens. According to FOX News, undocumented immigrants are snatching up all of the best jobs these days. Then they asked for my social security number to run, they told me, a "credit check." Of course I have bad credit. That's why I need a job. I wouldn't be begging for the privilege of handling toxic pesticides and bug zappers had I multiple offshore accounts in the Caymans.

Under the Microscope

I've worked for roughly one company my entire adult life. It did not require I produce DNA samples, pee in a cup, or jump through psychological hoops to

118

demonstrate my emotional soundness. Maybe it wished it had.

Home Giant's application, on the other hand, included a number of tests to measure my emotional intelligence. Seriously, if I had even a scintilla of emotional intelligence, do you think I'd be opening my life to judgment by a store that sells waterless urinals? I was peppered with a cluster of questions that asked me to rate my general human condition against that of my "friends"—traits including honesty, happiness, cleanliness, industriousness and optimism. One after another, I was asked if I was "more than, less than, or equal to" a particular quality. Was I cleaner? Was I more productive? Was I sunnier, brighter and more absorbent than my band of brothers? Did I consider myself as respectful, as tolerant, or as gentle on the environment as my cohorts?

You have to remember that most of my friends are in a program of recovery with varying lengths of sobriety. These people are as equally capable of going on a killing spree as running the nation on any given day. Saying I believed I'm smarter than my friends might sound arrogant, while answering that I'm less compassionate might have me come across as a sociopath. I've worked my whole life to be better than the next guy, could I dare be thought of as simply satisfactory? What did these diabolical HR directors want from me? They should have talked directly to my friends or sponsor and cut me completely out of the process.

Then came questions to assess my actual "handiness." Could I swing a hammer? Have I ever worked with pneumatic tools? And, if yes, please rate my expertise from "little" to "expert." What was I to say? Can't the hiring managers extrapolate that if I've spent the last 25 years behind a desk writing press releases about biodegradable cars I probably haven't been installing too many sump pumps? I was actually asked my toilet installation aptitude. Were they actually going to call me in for an interview to see if I showed up wearing a tool belt and pants exposing my butt crack? Betting they wouldn't, I instantly became an on-paper expert in mixing cement, soldering copper pipe, flash metal roofing and junction box wiring. Truth be told, I can't even drive a nail straight or get a fork out of the garbage disposal without my partner's help.

The assessment concluded with the infamous, "What would you do" questions. In this section I was asked to read a list of hypothetical scenarios and then choose the answer I believed most closely matched the action I'd take.

An example: You notice that one of your co-workers is stealing. Would you a) join in the heist; b) pretend you didn't notice and continue working; c) report the employee to the store manager; d) go on break; e) tackle the employee to the ground.

There were a lot of stealing questions—customers, employees, managers—along with situations dealing with unhappy people, like this one: An irate customer claims the store has run out of an advertised sale item. Would you a) offer them a rain check; b) pretend you didn't notice and continue working; c) try to sell them a higher priced item instead; d) go on break; e) tackle the customer to the ground.

Here's a news flash for Home Giant. There is only one answer to every "what would you do" question in every circumstance since the beginning of time. The answer: I have no fucking idea. My personal experience tells me that unless you are actually in the situation—right in the cross hairs—you have no idea what the hell you'd do. The people who say, "I would have jumped into the gorge to save the baby, disarmed the terrorist with the bomb, given half the $50-million lottery winnings to charity and turned off the free porn" are full of shit.

Don't Call Us, Ever

Once the application was completed, I was told it would be saved in the company's database for 60 days. Like after two months I'd go back and repeat that fresh hell.

Ultimately, I didn't make the hiring cut. And while I know I shouldn't, I often ponder what Home Giant was looking for in an ideal employee. Did it really matter that I said I'd help the guy in the next department once my work was done? Did they expect me to be a one-man crime stopper? Can anyone really estimate drywall measurements in their head? And what is a spinner tool?

What can a company—paying minimum wage, offering crappy hours and no benefits—really hope for in a worker? At best, I believe, are employees who are honest and polite to customers, show up on time, do their work and occasionally bathe. That sounds like me. But since it wasn't, who did win the Home Giant employment marathon? Who is so pure or so smart or can lie so well as to pass the 195-question test? Who among us hasn't shoplifted a lip gloss, or gets confused when given Canadian currency, or wouldn't lose their shit if a hypothetical customer hijacked a carload of copper pipe fittings—whatever they are?

And can do it all drug free?

Misery Loves Company

To assuage my feelings of inferiority, I searched the Internet for kindred Home Giant flunkouts. Apparently I wasn't alone. Thousands of us slackers were posting about our experiences—the intrusiveness, the disrespect, the shame, the pee. It appears that few are called to wear the elusive crimson smock. The rest of us just sit around and write crappy things about those who are. That's what I call the American way.

So without the mettle necessary to join the Giant, I continued looking for work, competing against the likes of unemployed colleagues Sarah Palin and Rosie O'Donnell. I'm in the same employment pool as the ex-

International Monetary Fund guy, the former voices of Elmo and the Aflac duck, and the space shuttle Endeavour.

My sponsor tells me that rejection—jobs, girlfriends, the Catholic Church—is God's protection. In that case, God's protected me from all types of employment—the usual public relations positions as well as new careers in zoo keeping and bank management. I've failed as a greeting-card writer, community college instructor— even the opportunity to pet sit an 18 month-old collie named Olivia. It's like living in an impenetrable employment condom.

As a result, I have resentments against the Obama administration, everyone who's currently employed or economically "comfortable," people asking to see my college transcripts, every career networking site, and especially Chelsea Handler, who has a TV show in addition to her three *New York Times* best-selling books. And she still gets to drink. Apparently, a lot.

When my list of resentments starts reading like the American Recovery and Reinvestment Act of 2009, I know it's time to reconnect with my higher power.

"Okay, God," I prayed. "I'm getting a lot of feedback on the jobs you don't want me to have. How about a clue as to what I should be doing for a living?"

God always answers my prayers. And I usually misinterpret Him.

Badly.

In the Beginning Was "The Word"

Quite by accident, I came across a job posting by K. Rupert Murdoch, CEO of News Corporation. The opening was for Director of Public Relations at Zondervan, a media and publishing subsidiary of Murdoch's vast, publicly traded global media conglomerate. In addition to being the world's largest publisher of bibles, Zondervan produces every type of Christian media imaginable and has been doing it successfully for 75 years. So successfully, it was gobbled up by Murdoch's HarperCollins division, famous for publishing *How to Make Love Like a Porn Star*, *The Satanic Bible*, and *The New Joy of Gay Sex*. Apparently by acquiring Zondervan, Mr. Murdoch was covering his spiritual bases.

The job itself looked promising, bringing together two of the things I like most, God and books. Okay, books are not among the top two things I like most, but I do like books somewhat. And these weren't just any books. These were blockbusters. Zondervan's the *Purpose Driven Life*, at 25 million copies, is the best-selling hardback book in American history. *The Case for Christ*, another of Zondervan's home runs, hit #1 on the bestseller list, sold 600,000 copies in its first 18 months and created an entire franchise of "Case for..." titles and study guides.

By spreading the word of God, Zondervan was making Mr. Murdoch a wealthier soul. Not that there's anything wrong with it. I love capitalism and the First

Amendment more than the next guy. Perhaps those are my two favorite things. No, it's still naps and the smell of wet dogs. Or bratwurst and college football.

I prayed to God and consulted with my usual earth-bound spiritual advisors on what to do next. The answer seemed obvious. Wasn't it God that brought my faith and vocation together in this one tidy offering? Wasn't it the opportunity of a lifetime to do His work? Wasn't working for HarperCollins a sure way to get my own "quasi-spiritual" book published? Believing I was on sound spiritual footing, I agreed to meet with the bible people for an interview. I thought I knew what I was getting into. Then again, I'm sure the folks at Zondervan thought the same thing.

Let Us Pray

Zondervan is headquartered in Grand Rapids, Michigan—home of Dick DeVos and Focus on the Family. I wasn't fooled into thinking I was going to the Castro. I braced myself for a day of right-wing Christian zeal—women with high hair and an infectious "Up With People" attitude. I expected some blurring between the secular and non-secular at Zondervan. What I hadn't expected, upon entering its majestic corporate office, was a life-size sculpture of Jesus Christ in bronze washing his disciple Peter's feet.

And that was just the beginning.

After meeting Jesus and Peter in the lobby, I was ushered into the cafeteria for lunch with Chris

Christiansen, VP of Zondervan's trade books division. We ordered deli sandwiches and walked to a private conference room for the interview.

"Before we get started, Charlotte," Chris said in earnest, "let's take care of the most important matter first."

Excellent, I thought. A real "nuts-and-bolts" guy. We were going to talk turkey or pastrami or whatever his luncheon meat du jour. Perhaps it was the matter of my obscene salary or enormous office or how we would transform lost souls, one share of stock at a time. He was, after all, one of Mr. Murdoch's disciples as well as God's.

Before I could open my yap, Chris closed his eyes, bowed his head and offered me his hand in prayer.

"Thank you, oh Lord, for Your bountiful gifts," he began. "Thank You for the food that nourishes our bodies and the many blessings that feed our soul. Thank You for bringing Charlotte to us safely in Your tender care. Watch over us and guide us today as we seek to do Thy will always."

In all of my job interviews, business luncheons, happy hours and annual performance appraisals—that was the first that began with an invocation.

"Well, that was nice," I attempted to convince myself inwardly. "And not at all awkward. Praying is, well, nice. I do it at home and privately all the time. This will be a nice interview. This is a nice man. And he will treat me nicely. And I shouldn't be at all concerned that we are praying over a meal despite the fact that this is a publicly traded company and that we are likely breaking several employment laws regarding corporate hiring practices."

Amen.

The next part of the interview actually was very nice, with no devotionals at all. Chris told me how his job at Zondervan was the perfect marriage of his spirituality and business experience. How his former career of selling Pepperidge Farm Goldfish Crackers left him unfulfilled, and how he was now able to use his vast and impressive marketing talents to be a fisher of men, instead of seller of cheddar fish (which I learned are also available as graham crackers and low-fat pretzels).

Then we talked about the book business, which was also nice. I love business. I could talk about it all day, even without praying about it. We discussed how ebooks were changing the publishing world, Kindles and Nooks, emerging markets, branding and growth opportunities.

"Tell me about the authors you publish," I asked Chris, recovering quite nicely from the before-meal prayer. I was beginning to hit my usual unflappable interview stride.

I was told that Zondervan had a great diversity of voice in its trade books division. Nothing like the word diversity to get my attention. It's right up there with sex and pot pies. (Maybe those are my two favorite things.)

Chris listed legal thrillers, self-help books and stories for children—all published by Zondervan. There were books about discovering an adopted child's past, sports trivia, former President Jimmy Carter, the hoarding craze and Arnold Palmer's lessons on golf.

I was duly impressed with Zondervan's breadth and scope of literary offerings.

"That's quite a booklist," I said. "What other types of spiritual material do you publish?"

I was referencing inspirational books other than bibles. It is a fact many spiritual seekers today are shifting away from organized religion and looking to build an individual and intimate relationship with a higher power. Young and old are fed up with the hostile, political, disingenuous dogma of the church and are reinventing the spiritual experience for themselves. As bookshelves are growing with non-traditional and philosophical works, I was curious just how diverse Zondervan really was.

"As a global communications company," Chris answered proudly, "we publish works from around the world that represent the various currents within the evangelical mainstream of Christian faith and practice."

So much for diversity. The word began to wilt like the enchanted rose in Beauty and the Beast.

I'm guessing the "various currents" he referenced are as exotically divergent as French Vanilla, Extra Creamy Vanilla, Homemade Vanilla, Natural Vanilla and Vanilla Bean ice cream.

"But doesn't that impact your workforce?" I asked. "Surely not everyone here practices the same monotheistic Christ-centered religion?"

"Actually we do," Chris said to my astonishment. "And on Wednesday afternoons we convert the cafeteria over for worship service."

As I sat speechless, Chris brought our conversation to a definite close.

"While it would be against the law for me to say we wouldn't hire a person based on their religious beliefs, suffice it to say, if you were not of the evangelical Christian orthodoxy, you likely would not feel comfortable here."

And with those words, I heard the familiar sound of a door slamming—with me on the outside.

The rest of the interview went by in a blur, something something benefits, all Christian holidays off, something something catechism, blah blah blah, casual Good Fridays.

"By the way," Chris said, almost as an afterthought, "It says on your resume you wrote a book. What's it about?"

I handed him a copy of *Mackinac Bridge Jesus.*

And that's when I believe the nice interview with the nice man stopped being nice.

Seen on Bumper Sticker: "Don't Put Words in My Mouth" - GOD

It was a long and quiet ride back to my house, mentally replaying the interview with Chris. I've since recapped the Zondervan story to a few friends in an attempt to make some sense of it.

"People like that are just bullies," a program pal said to me kindly. "It's like he's saying, 'My God can beat up your God.' You know your God loves you. You don't need his."

I never heard back from the people at Zondervan, not a note thanking me for driving all the way to Grand Rapids, much less telling me I didn't get the job. Offering me $50 for gas seems like the evangelical Christian thing to do. I'm sure Jesus would have at least texted.

Perhaps I'll never know why I wasn't offered the job pitching God's good books. I'm hoping it was my spiritual ideology or my sexual orientation. I would hate to think that Mr. Murdoch called a few of my former employers and learned that I really do suck at PR.

In my subsequent research of Zondervan's titles, I found *Washed and Waiting*, a book discussing how "homosexuality goes against God's express will for all human beings."

Seems that would have been a good thing to learn before my 160 mile drive.

God's Will for $1,000 Please, Alex

I've come no closer to discovering God's big career plans for me. It continues to frustrate me and even question God's motivation in creating these employment challenges.

"People think God tests them," says my therapist Diane. "This is not true. He presents learning opportunities. Think of it like shopping for a new suit. You get to try on as many as you'd like. Each one feels different. After a while, you begin to notice things—the material, how they are cut, how they make you feel, if there's room to grow. You've been trying on a lot of suits, Charlotte. You're beginning to trust yourself to make a good choice—when the right suit comes along."

I hope it will soon.

Right now, the only thing that fits is my pajamas.

TLL

Insanity

I met a guy the other day who identified himself as a recreational heroin user.

Hmmm, I thought to myself, I wonder what that looks like? I've known recreational boaters. They're usually obnoxious people who decorate their homes in nautical themes, dress like the skipper on Gilligan's Island, and use words like gunwale and jibsheet.

I'm not quite sure how "recreational" relates to the use of heroin. I guess it refers to his amateur status. Most of the folks I know hooked on that junk leave the nonprofessional ranks very quickly. It's not like they're afraid of getting disqualified from the Olympics.

Do these people have other pastimes, like collecting miniature lighthouses? Whittling? Hosting home parties for jewelry or candles or knock-off purses? Would they hang out with the same fun-loving socialites known as recreational serial killers, recreational prostitutes and recreational pedophiles? What would be these folks' full-time jobs?

I believe qualifying yourself as a recreational heroin user has less to do with avocation and more to do with insanity. But what do I know? I'm a recreational lesbian.

Seriously, what else would you call a person who sticks a needle filled with poison in his or her body multiple times a day while thinking, "This is a really good idea?" I think "insane" is as apt a characterization as any.

Each of us is likely insane in someone's eyes. That's the great thing about insanity. Like pornography, we all know it when we see it.

Here are testimonials from people I would label insane:

"Some of my friends and I thought it would be fun to cut the legs off an old ironing board and use it to surf down the staircase in our dorm. We knocked out the railing and a big hunk of drywall before going to the hospital."

"I thought I made a sexy booty call to my boyfriend late one night only to find out the next day I had actually drunk dialed my mother."

"Because we didn't have a car, I jumped in a grocery cart and my buddy pushed me to the drive-up teller at the bank, after which we were arrested."

"For no reason, I threw a hard-boiled egg out the window of my moving car and hit a stranger in the face going about 45 mph."

"My friend stuck one of those suction-cup cat toys to her forehead, passed out, and woke up the next morning in a pool of blood and synthetic bird feathers."

There is one common theme in these stories besides insanity. Can you guess? That's right; alcohol played a role—probably the lead.

Being in recovery, I've heard too many of these stories. In fact, some people like to brag about just how insane they've been. One guy I know explained how he couldn't get "drunk enough" on conventional liquor, so he began drinking vanilla extract. This is a product required by law to be at least 35 percent alcohol. Another man thought himself a genius when he filled his car's windshield-washer reservoir with vodka and routed the hose into the passenger compartment through an air vent. One new mother was so crazed for a fix she took her newborn into a crack house, but claimed the baby was safe because the shack was surrounded by men with machine guns.

The Windy Alcoholic

My favorite insanity story is courtesy of Chicago Bob, a man who speaks regularly at the rehab facility I attended. Each month, Bob holds his audience rapt in attention like Girl Scouts around a camp fire. Bob is part lawyer, part stand-up comic, part evangelist. His story is a fantastic roller coaster ride filled with manic highs and harrowing lows.

According to his tale, Bob started life as street punk running dope on the south side of Chicago. He triumphantly redeemed himself, earning a law degree, building a lucrative practice and collecting the trappings of success. But in a very *Leaving Las Vegas* way, he bottomed out, "shitting in pizza boxes in (his) $5 million condo on Lake Shore Drive." I don't know why that particular part of his story sticks in my head, but it had the appropriate shock value I'm sure he intended. Of course, Bob's story ends with his miraculous recovery—like a phoenix with an off-shore bank account. His stellar return to prosperity left the audience duly impressed, if not exhausted. He had it all, lost it all, and—through the blessings of the 12-steps (and a proficient hedge-fund manager) was back atop the world and there to crow about it.

I must confess, it was some story.

Fortunately for me, I'm not as awed with Bob's type of insanity as I once was. I can relate more closely to the people with the ironing board and the cat toy. My using life was never as Hollywood-worthy as Bob's, nor do I measure my recovery in dollars and cents. It's okay though, we're told in the program to relate to each other—not compare. I met a former nurse in the same rehab facility who helped carry a dead body from a crack house to a nearby swamp. I've never done that either—thank God—but I can relate to the insanity that got her into that situation.

"The belief I can drink like other people," is my insanity. The truth is I never wanted to drink like other people. What the hell fun would that be? Those were the real loons, the people who would order one beer, or worse, nurse a vodka tonic the whole evening and leave half of it in a glass of melting ice. Those were the ones who needed to be locked up or forced into a weekend "Alcohol Awareness" class. What do they drink with sushi, a Mountain Dew? That's criminal.

During my drinking and drugging, I used a number of tricks to convince myself I could manage my own insanity. I vowed to only drink on certain days of the week. That extended to days only ending in the letters "d-a-y."

It makes no impact on my addiction what conditions I concoct once I put that first drink or drug in my body. After that first hit, it doesn't matter if I'm drinking cooking sherry or Stolichnaya out of a sippy cup. It's insanity to think I have any control at all over my addiction.

People define insanity as doing the same thing over and over and expecting a different result. That pegs an alcoholic. Who else would say, "Last time I drank I got a DUI, ran over my neighbor's cat, my wife filed for divorce and I vomited in the toaster. Let's see what happens when I do it again tonight."

Stupid is as Stupid Does

I was shocked when I learned my insanity and my addiction were not entirely related. That is to say, I can be—and often am—still insane without using. For example: I slept with a woman in rehab (sober) and was crushed to learn she wasn't "the one." Out of desperation, I begged my ex-husband to take me back a year after our divorce was final. I was more than two years sober (and still pretty gay) when I pulled that move. Even today—more than 10 years clean—I'm still out of my mind. Just ask my sponsor and the IRS.

I once said to my sister, "I thought when I got sober I'd stop being so stupid." Her reply was, "Really? Not me."

There are still times today when being crazy feels normal to me—when doing the sane thing feels foreign—like the homeless guy who has slept on the streets so long he can't get comfortable in a real bed. It's when I yell at the automated phone system about my cable bill or spend two hours trying to download the Meow Mix jingle as my ringtone. When I order Snuggies for everyone on our Christmas gift list, or I allow other people to determine my self-worth, I know the circus is still in town.

Big Tobacco

While perhaps not entirely Christian, I'm glad I'm not alone on my frequent visits to crazy town. My recovery friend Vicki recently found herself there while having her kitchen redone. Having been through two kitchen remodels myself, I'm familiar with the insanity that can accompany the process. In our house, like in most homes, the kitchen is the heart of the body. It's where everything happens—people congregate, food is prepared, dishes are cleaned, animals are fed, paperwork stacks up. As such, when the heart is transplanted, everyone feels uprooted and crabby. The daily routine is shot to hell. You end up eating your meals standing on the bed; feeding the cats on the toilet seat; and putting mail under the cushions of the living room sofa. No wonder we didn't pay our bills for four months.

Remodeling is a process that can't be completed fast enough, and one you can't believe you had the bad sense to undertake. I felt Vicki's pain the moment she said the word "contractor"—which is a growth moment for me. I'm glad I can have empathy for someone who has $10,000 lying around for granite counter tops when my paycheck barely covers cat litter and ramen noodles.

Vicki told us she was holding it pretty well together, using all of the tools in her spiritual tool box. That includes praying, taking long walks, going to a lot of meetings, trying to stay out of the process and handing it over to God. That is, until the electrician showed up.

"That's when I knew I was going to lose it," she admitted. "I started counting his smoking breaks. I'm washing out pickle jars in the powder room and he's lighting up every seven to ten minutes. His cough was like a metronome, it never missed a beat. I wanted to choke him to death!"

Unfortunately, the electrician was doing a good job of that himself—he had already puffed himself down to one remaining lung. But that didn't stop him. Into his lone lung and without the benefit of a mask, he inhaled the dust and mold and Lord knows what else of Vicki's kitchen, along with an unfiltered Camel cigarette about eight times an hour.

"I doubt," said Vicki, "that had I been able to stop him for just one minute, look him directly in the eyes and ask point blank, 'Do you think this is a good idea?' he would have said, 'Yes.' I think the nicotine made him nuts."

After his lung operation, I bet Mr. Electrician was one of those guys with his ass hanging out of his hospital gown, hooked up to his IV standing in the snow, puffing like a diesel engine.

Let's All Try the Two Step

"Came to believe that a power greater than myself could restore me to sanity," is a paramount tenet in my recovery program. Some days I believe it, some days I don't. That in itself is insanity. How can one day I believe something with the very core of my being, and the next day have total amnesia? I'm like a bad soap opera actress.

I believe God always is. I just pretend sometimes He isn't. Keeping separate from God allows me to practice my insanity. I find that comforting from time to time. After having lived there so long, I occasionally miss it. Like visiting the old, run-down neighborhood. I guess that's what happens to parents when their kids finally move out of the house. After years and years of chaos and yelling and stereo speakers and drum sets, the quiet nearly kills them. I hear many of them take up clog dancing.

Many people in the program of recovery say they were never sane to start with. I can relate to that. According to a recent medical study, the average adult human has 35,000 discrete thoughts in a day. Alcoholics, in comparison, have one thought 35,000 times daily.

The cure for insanity? I think it must come in small doses. If my insanity was removed immediately and completely—all in one swoop—I'd get the bends. Thankfully, God has removed some of it. I'm not drinking or drugging. I no longer get crazy in traffic. My insane concern over what the world thinks of me is waning. My sponsor says, "What other people think of me is none of my business." I don't practice that perfectly, but the good news is most of the time I don't really give a shit.

Shots, the Hard Way

Depending on your age, your image of insanity was shaped by Joanne Woodward in *The Three Faces of Eve*, Jack Nicholson in *One Flew Over the Cuckoo's Nest* or Wynona Ryder in *Girl, Interrupted*. But rarely is insanity so obvious, humorous, attractive or Oscar worthy.

Insanity is lurking all around us, not just in the addict population. I know a lot of non-alcoholics who can't stop eating potato chips, can't turn off QVC, gamble away their IRAs or can't say no to sex. I know a lot of people who simply can't say no.

Insanity made up 75 percent of Jay Leno's nightly monologue. He joked about a burglar so vain he sent police his updated photo after his plastic surgery. We all laugh at the annual Darwin Awards, which commemorate people who improve the gene pool by eliminating themselves from it. A recent nominee set off a firecracker from atop his head and died. A winner died of alcohol poisoning after having two 1.5 liter bottles of sherry inserted into his anus. I would not want to be his bartender.

Despite our societal evolution where topics like consequences and compulsive behavior and addiction are discussed openly in classrooms and on the couches of talk shows, we'll likely not rid ourselves of insanity any time soon. Especially when our Hollywood heroes include Lindsay Lohan and Charlie Sheen. I doubt insanity is anywhere more rampant than in our government. Election 2016: Need I say more?

Give Him the Chair

Perhaps we can't eradicate insanity, but we can develop a good sense of humor. Maybe being human means being a little nuts. I'll expect insanity to continue in every segment of our lives and I'm prepared to see stories like this one, a personal favorite:

"Dennis LeRoy Anderson, 62, from Proctor, Minnesota, pleaded guilty to a DWI involving a homemade motorized La-Z-Boy. The incident occurred when—returning home after a long visit to the neighborhood watering hole—

Anderson's lounge chair hit a parked vehicle. At the time of the incident, Anderson had a blood-alcohol content of 0.29%, more than three times the legal limit. Anderson claims he was driving the chair 'fine' until a woman jumped on it and knocked the chair off course. Anderson's recliner was powered by a converted lawnmower engine and featured a custom stereo system, cup holders and National Hot Rod Racing Association stickers. As a result of the DWI, Anderson's chair was confiscated and will be auctioned off."

Auctioned off?

If doing the same thing over again and expecting a different result is insanity, perhaps the recliner should be retired and sent to the Darwin Award judges or, better yet, any member of Congress.

TLL

Mommy, is Eddie a Gay?

We believe that only one of our many pets is gay.

All have been fixed except baby Sophia, who arrived at the house the size of a Dixie Riddle cup and for some reason continues to escape the knife.

Without working reproductive organs, I'm told our animals are no longer sexually active, regardless of their mating preference. And yet, I still find our 78-pound dog Tobi humping Mr. Nibbles, our supersized black cat. We often catch our female dog in the act of licking Tobi's winkie—a sight more disturbing than I can describe. Wainwright—our orange tom—has a crush on Tobi's enormous toy turtle, and is frequently seen hoisting the plush faux reptile from room to room, followed by the sound of passionate squeaking.

The vet says all of this behavior is more about dominance in the pack than anyone's libido at work. I really don't care, as long as no one gets hurt. As Tina says, "What's love got to do with it?"

Princess Eddie the First

Edgar, however, is quite another story.

Edgar is a queen.

To quote a favorite Seinfeld line: "Not that there's anything wrong with that."

143

Edgar is the Liberace of cats. He minces and preens. He has a neatly groomed and luscious pelt. He likes to slap at things and wear sweaters. He is thin and tidy and keeps his toys—all pastel and made of sparkles and bright feathers—well organized in a wicker basket. He can be distant and aloof one minute, and engaging the next. He nestles for afternoon naps deep in Tobi's underbelly pretending it's a fur-lined cape. There's definitely something wrong with animals wearing other animals.

Edgar enjoys sitting upright on a chair at the dining room table while Sharon and I have supper. He's a great dinner companion. He listens in wide-eyed fascination to our conversations—head swiveling back and forth as if watching center court at Wimbledon. Then he runs like a ball boy to grab a speck of meat off my plate with great satisfaction. I often imagine him adding his two-cents to the discussion—gossip about who hoards food or stinks up the litter box or steals all the mouse toys. Edgar would be great to lunch with, to shop with, to take to the community pool in his miniature Speedo and criticize the overweight residents and their ill-behaved children. Edgar is Joan Rivers without the plastic surgery or annoying daughter. If he were one of Santa's reindeer, Edgar would definitely be Prancer, perhaps on a team with Lisper, Flamer and Kyle.

We're All a Bunch of Animals

That Edgar is gay and also a cat is apparently not news. At least not to Jon Mooallem, author of, "Can Animals be Gay?" —an in-depth article that appeared in *The New York Times Magazine.*

The simple answer to the seemingly rhetorical question is, "Yes."

But as we all know, rarely are things ever that simple.

Mr. Mooallem's tale of animal sexual orientation begins with a below-the-beak look at life for the Laysan albatross. The birds, which can live well past 50, mate for life. They are definitely monogamous. But heterosexual? Not so much. According to Lindsay Young, a leading researcher who conducted a comprehensive study of the birds, roughly one-third of the pairings that nest at Hawaii's Kaena Point are female-only couples. They incubate, rear, nuzzle and groom the same as male-female couples, with no tell-tale signs of feather mullets or flannel shirts to give them away. By all accounts, the same-sex couples mix into the flock, flying under the radar, so to speak.

The findings of Young's lengthy study created a political storm—in and out of the scientific community. Young's results were hailed as either the missing proof in the fight for same-sex equality or "pure propaganda and selective science at its dumbest." Senator Tom Coburn (R-OK) requested the Feds pull Young's research funding, despite the fact the government wasn't picking up her tab. Funnyman Stephen Colbert called the birds "albatresbians that threatened American family values with their Sappho-avian agenda." A gay-rights group requested a rainbow flag be flown above each female-female nest in solidarity.

Young herself doesn't stereotype animals as either gay or straight, saying those terms are reserved for humans. She reiterated that her task was to study the albatross—sexual activity being only *one* of its many characteristics. How people mistakenly extrapolated the data and misrepresented it for profit, she said, was their own sad doing.

A big mistake many people made was assuming that Young herself was gay, and that her sexual orientation played some role in her findings. She is not. I believe it is offensive to suggest Young, a respected scientist, arrived at her conclusions because she was a lesbian, and a manipulating one at that. Instead, she should be credited with having extraordinary avian gaydar.

Birds of a Feather Sleep Together

"What animals do—what's perceived to be 'natural,'" Mooallem wrote in his article, "seems to carry a strange moral potency: it's out there, irrefutably, as either a validation or a denunciation of our own (human) behavior, depending on how you happen to feel about homosexuality and about nature."

Before you discredit Mr. Mooallem's theory, look at a newspaper. A male penguin couple in the San Diego

Zoo made global headlines when, after six years together, one flew the coop to be with a female. In a ridiculous scandal, the zoo's penguin keeper was accused of separating the pair in some type of heterosexual conspiracy. Another male penguin pair, featured in the book *And Tango Makes Three*, tells how a male couple raised a chick together. The book ruffled the feathers of Christian right groups like Focus on the Family, which said the book promoted a left-wing political agenda. I didn't know penguins had agendas, left-wing or otherwise.

I've never looked to my pets for the gold standard of behavior. Nor do I attempt to argue or define what is meant by normal. Driving eight blocks to the 7-Eleven for a morning coffee is very normal. But that's for me, certainly not for my dog. But then, normal for him is eating breakfast hot out of the litter box.

Is it Really All About the Nasty?

Eminent naturalist, geologist and biologist Charles Darwin contended that all behavior was geared toward only one thing: reproduction. It was also believed he suffered from extreme mental illness. This guy must have been a real lady charmer. Could you imagine his opening line on a date? "How about dinner, a movie and a little unprotected coitus?"

If Mr. Darwin's theory is correct—that life is solely about propagating the species—why are scientists outting God's creatures at a record pace? What are all these flaming flamingos, bison, beetles, guppies and warthogs doing on the down low? According to Uncle Charles, these animals should by now be deselected from the gene pool, unable to pass along all the same-sex DNA they're bursting with. And yet they exist. Male dolphins are invading each other's blowholes, female koalas are mounting each other, and male orangutans are fellating each other, and not just for the nutritional value.

Gays With Benefits

Perhaps all the non-reproducing mammals add something of value besides sperm and eggs to the recipe. Perhaps homosexual and heterosexual behavior, as one scientist suggests, are not tidy opposites. Perhaps what we perceive to be homosexual sex in the animal world isn't about sex at all. After all, someone has to decorate the jungle and teach all the other animals how to play softball.

Dr. Mengele, Line One

There exists in the world of science and morality those who wish to eradicate gays altogether. Their quest is the gay chromosome—the holy grail of DNA. If found, society could re-engineer everyone's genes to fit today's populist notion of normal—the union of one man and one woman. Sounds like a bad Tom Cruise movie.

I'm not a proponent of trampling anywhere on God's domain. Are we really so sure God screwed up when He made homosexuals? And who wants to be the one to bring that to His attention? My therapist continues to tell me God doesn't make garbage.

Online Mail Bag

Mr. Mooallem's article was informative, intelligent and written with just the right touch of tongue-in-cheek social commentary. But the best part by far was the online feedback posted on the magazine's website. The 416 responses were generally divided into four camps—pro-gay, anti-gay, those saying the article was basically stupid and a waste of time, and those outraged that the article ran on Easter Sunday. Among my favorites:

"Have the religious Right rewritten the biology books yet again?"

"We are what we are; there is no right or wrong way between consenting adults or birds."

"If these scientists want to make a genuine contribution, maybe they can tell us why we Westerners are so hung up on erotic pleasure."

"This is the dumbest article ever."

"I think it (homosexuality) is a manufacturing defect. Just like some people are born with genetical defects in eyes and limbs, I think gay people are born with genetical defects in their sexual orientation assembly."

"Duh. One of my pet birds is madly in love with another male bird. We also have a breeding pair whose female spends more time grooming the object of the gay bird's affection. Go figure."

"For anyone who insists on consulting the natural world for guidance on behavior, I recommend looking for evidence of fag-bashing. Have any of these biologists observed heterosexual animals 'punishing' members of their own species who deviate from their personal sexual norms? If not, human moral busybodies should take the hint that God has given us through nature and mind their own business."

"I suspect animals couldn't care less whether their behavior condemns or condones human activity—they would probably just rather be left alone."

"WE ARE EVERYWHERE!"

You May Seek Other Options

Recently, the unconventional albatross made news again—this time in New Zealand. A female "couple" plus a male albatross was spotted presiding over a single nest. Some researchers called it "just another alternative mating strategy." I call it a 1970s sitcom starring Suzanne Somers.

Apparently more and more of these atypical natural couplings are being discovered in nature; further proving the notion that heterosexual and homosexual behavior are not tidy opposites. Nor do these two distinctions represent all of nature's mating configurations.

I wish scientists would have told me that years ago.

I was about nine or ten years into my marriage when I started seeing a lesbian therapist for the sole purpose of divining my sexual orientation. Up until that time I had had only two lovers—my female college roommate and my husband. Like the albatross, both were long-term monogamous relationships. Unlike the birds, however, I had a deep desire to be straight.

I had been raised to believe that homosexuality was not simply an "alternative mating strategy"—but instead sinful and wrong and taboo. I believed it.

My therapist was the size of a side-by-side refrigerator and wore a retractable keychain on her belt. I was a whiny, self-indulgent housewife who lusted after straight chicks in tank tops.

Needless to say, we did not hit it off. She diagnosed my situation in 90 seconds.

"It's too good to leave, too bad to stay," she said of my marriage.

She was right. I didn't want to leave for a million obvious reasons. And I didn't want to stay for a million others.

"There are more than two options," she said to me in our last meeting that came just six weeks after our first. "It's not just about staying or leaving. There are any number of alternatives you can explore."

For the life of me I couldn't think of even one.

"You can stay in your marriage," she stated, as if about to rattle off the U.S. presidents in chronological order, "and take a mistress. Your husband could also take a mistress. The two of you could share one. You could have an open marriage, you could swing, he could be your beard, you could have separate personal lives but stay married for financial and appearance purposes.

You could buy an apartment for sexual liaisons. You can be bi-sexual."

I think the list went on for some time. I lost consciousness after the word "alternatives."

Talk about your sexual bumpkin. Most of what she said was completely foreign to me. Maybe they spoke like that in the land of Sophisticated People, but for me her words held no meaning. I had heard some of her references in R-rated movies and dirty jokes. But I was seeing this therapist to find a way *not* to be sexually perverse, not for help in writing letters to Penthouse.

I couldn't grasp any of her suggestions as plausible for me. I was so uptight that pretty much any sex—generic and spelled with a small "s"—freaked me out. At the end of the session, I ran from her office as if I had accidentally found my parents "doing it" right on her couch.

Standard Deviation

Maybe Mr. Mooallem is right. Maybe there is no one set of right answers that explain behavior—sexual or otherwise. Maybe messy and confusing and heartbreaking and curious and glorious is exactly the way Mother Nature intended. Somewhere along the way we made it our job to figure everything out. Maybe there are parts of the magic trick that should stay hidden.

When my best friend's daughter was no older than eight, she spotted a bird's nest in the family's backyard.

Two female robins were cohabitating—feathering and gathering and tooting happily together.

"Mom," Claire said confidently without inflection, "there are two lesbian birds living in our tree."

That said, she returned to her art project and after-school snack.

Merely an observation.

TLL

Anne Lamott Kissed My Coin

A stranger gave me a gift today. While I'm willing to say it was unexpected, I wasn't exactly surprised. Few things in life really surprise me anymore, now that I've learned God's in charge. All of the things I once believed coincidental and near impossibilities are simply God at work, sometimes behind the curtain, but most of the time right before my eyes. Don't get me wrong, I don't take His handiwork for granted. But it is nice to know my life isn't just some random drive-by shooting.

Earlier this month I volunteered to give an open talk at one of my regular 12-step meetings. To be honest, I didn't so much volunteer. I raised my hand to wave at my sponsor to indicate where I was sitting—she had arrived late—at the exact moment the meeting leader asked, "Is anyone here willing to give an open talk on the last Friday of this month?" Thank God I wasn't at a Christie's auction. I might have accidentally bought Johnny Cash's San Quentin prison jumpsuit for $1.5 million.

As hilarious as it was, I was still on the hook. Now that I have a couple talks under my belt, I don't fret about them like I used to. I do as my sponsor instructs, "Ask God for the words," and usually no one gets hurt.

I spoke about a subject I've been harping a lot on lately: "Going to any lengths." I want to be more than just clean and sober, I want to be happy. Insanely happy, to be honest. So I must be, as my program instructs, willing to go to any lengths to help make that happen.

What I spoke about was neither radical nor remarkable. Just some things I try to practice to get me closer to—if not nirvana—a better me. It's common sense, really, which can be pretty illusive among alcoholics.

I believe these ideas are important for me—and possibly everyone else on earth—to consider every day:

Brush my teeth—I've never found any long-term answers hiding under my covers. So if I'm brushing my teeth, it likely means I've gotten out of bed and I'm embarking on joining the living. Some days that alone is an accomplishment. Once I'm up, I can muster the momentum to do human things like eat protein, open my mail and vacuum. Already, I'm on track to being a productive citizen. I have a sign in my bathroom that reads: Plug in, be part of the solution, don't procrastinate and pick up after the dogs. As I brush I feel better about myself. And my dentist loves me.

Stop and ask for directions—I've yet to meet anyone with quality, long-term sobriety who's done it on their own. Recovery is a "we" program. As such, I must ask for help—I just can't wait around for someone to rescue me. I believe God will not do for me anything I can do for myself. And that's a lot. If I am willing, the rest is a piece of cake. Mmmmm. Cake.

Resist being an asshole—I can't expect other people not to be assholes if I'm leading by example. Resentment and anger don't bring about world peace. Flipping off the driver next to me doesn't introduce good karma. If I'm being a jerk off, I'm certainly not practicing acceptance, gratitude, humility, restraint, honesty, patience and serenity. I'm not that good at multitasking. As I shed my asshole self, I feel others around me doing the same until they become so rare I can barely recognize them. And vice versa.

Turn off the TV—When I stopped using drugs I immediately turned to other types of self-destructive and addictive behavior, partly because I was bored, but mostly because I had no idea who I was. I didn't want to be left alone with the person who frightened me most—me. Swapping one addiction for another isn't sober behavior. I had to learn the phrase, "Put the cupcakes down, walk away and no one gets hurt." That also works for Netflix, Facebook, Words With Friends, ESPN and every cat video on YouTube.

Do what the sign says—If the sign reads, "Stop," it means I must stop. If it reads, "No left turn," it means, "Charlotte, it is not legal for *you* to turn left. Period." That it is more convenient for me to do otherwise, that I'm running late, that there appears to be no police cruiser in sight does not matter. The sign is there for me—not just for you other people. Somehow telling myself that I can bend the rules leads me to a drink. I don't know exactly how it happens. It starts with the belief I'm unique. Being unique is the quickest way to rationalize that drinking or drugging makes sense for me, because God knows, "If you had my problems, you'd drink, too." Paying attention to the street sign makes me a man among men—no better than—no worse than, and certainly not unique. I add a little something to every road sign I see—"This Means ME!"

Don't talk to people who aren't there—My best thinking told me that drugging and drinking would make my problems go away. My best thinking told me God didn't love me. My best thinking told me I could hide from who I was. Clearly, my best thinking sucks. So, every once in awhile, I need to get out of my own head and talk with a real, live person. If I'm in a room alone, yelling at dead people or institutions or situations that aren't really about me, I'm fucked. I must live in the present, take responsibility for my own actions and let go of my resentments. And say goodbye to the imaginary people. They don't pay rent, anyway.

Be afraid—This doesn't mean go to corn mazes or haunted houses or look at my bank statement. It simply means I must be willing to walk into my fears, instead of doing everything humanly possible to dodge them. Let's face it, they're going to get me sooner or later. Like pulling off a Band-Aid, quicker is better. Things have never turned out as badly as I imagined they would. If I get a queasy feeling in my stomach, I know there is an important life lesson waiting just around the bend. If I'm willing to do things differently—like practice gratitude and humility—those pesky demons are no match for me. I find fear vanishes as faith enters—although sometimes fear is so fat it gets stuck in the door frame on its way out, making it almost impossible for faith to wiggle through.

Always say, "thank you"—For me, going to any length means: Show appreciation. Don't touch things that don't belong to me. Be optimistic (even if it kills me). Apologize when the situation calls for it. Help one person every day. Don't be a baby. Pray my ass off. And above all, never give up. Even after the miracle happens.

The Miracle is You

Once I got all of those words out of my system, I thanked everyone for listening, which is the audience's cue to wake up. I walked over to the refreshment table to get a Styrofoam cup of water. My mouth gets awfully dry after all that yapping. That's when I received my gift. A woman who I'd never met walked up to me, dug into her change purse, removed a medallion bearing the likeness of Mother Teresa, kissed it and pressed it into my hand. She looked me in the eyes and thanked me for doing God's work. She then returned to her table and finished off a blueberry muffin the size of a baby Panda.

I wasn't surprised, but I was impressed. Not at my performance, mind you, but at God's constant and very active presence in my life. That simple exchange—the unknown woman's acknowledgement of me—was God's virtual noogie.

"You did good," God was saying to me. "You're on the right track. Now don't get a big head and continue to pay attention."

That was both my blessing and my assignment: Do as I say, give forth what's inside you and everything will be fine.

Sometimes I forget the last part—a shortcoming of being human, I guess. But I am starting to become aware of my part in God's big wacky plan: Give in gratitude and receive in humility.

The giving part is like being a kid at Christmas. When I was little, I gave inexpensive and hand-made gifts. They were small, cheap and of no measurable value. They were all I had and—like the little drummer boy—I gave them purely from the heart. So while I was giving clay ashtrays formed in the shape of my hand and $3.00 bottles of perfume that could clear a room, my parents were giving me trips to Disney World and bicycles and warm wool coats. I gave them just a little—grains of sand on the beach. They gave me the whole ocean in return.

That's God equation: whatever you give comes back $756(x)^4$—or something like it.

Don't get me wrong—I still have to push against the cynic in me—the skeptic who wants to poo-poo these episodes in my life. After all, the "medallion" was little more than a scrap of aluminum weighing less than a potato chip. Adding it to my chain would likely cause my skin to break out and my neck to turn green. And what do I really know of this "mysterious" lady? Perhaps she's some sort of lunatic with a stockpile of these holy pull tabs at home, like Schroeder with his closet full of Beethoven busts.

To allow the inexplicable wonder to manifest in my life, I must constantly reject my jaded self. The fact is I gave an alcoholic a few small words, and she gave me the Saint of Calcutta to watch over me. I'd say that was a pretty good deal.

Cleveland Rocks

Today's exchange reminded me of the last time a woman kissed a medallion and pressed it into my palm. I should more precisely say it reminded me of the only other time it happened—it's not like women shower me with trinkets and smooches on a daily basis. Just ask my partner.

I had just celebrated my one-year sobriety anniversary, and in recognition of the accomplishment my BFF Sharon took me to see Anne Lamott, my favorite author. This is the same best friend who flew me to rehab, taught me to pray and helped me to wear matching clothes that first year sober. She also invited me into her magical world of books, where I met many rich characters—real and imagined—and the men and women who gave them life. Like Sharon, Anne was instrumental in my getting sober, and was a great source of inspiration through the pages of *Traveling Mercies*, and later *Plan B* and *Grace (Eventually)*. While not a single mother living in California or a George Bush detractor or a woman with wildly self-defiant hair, I did find a connection with Anne. Through her wickedly funny and painfully tender words, Anne helped me accept my alcoholism, find a God of my understanding and learn to embrace myself. That I was going to hear her words in person seated next to my guardian angel was the greatest gift I could've imagined.

The book reading was held at Amasa Stone Chapel on the campus of Case Western Reserve University near Cleveland. Because the prearranged seats were held exclusively for members of the University's lecture series, Sharon and I were asked to wait outside the 100 year-old church until all the reserved seats were accounted for. Then the rest of us would be allowed in. What at first appeared to be an inconvenience turned out to be another of God's gifts.

It was a perfect day—clear and crisp—and ideal for making new friends. Sharon and I arrived early, allowing us plenty of time to get to know our fellow Anne fans. We met several lovely people in line—a hilarious married couple, three best friends and an entire book club. Two well dressed women with their college-aged daughters were determined to create the ultimate mother/daughter moment—one they would recall on their respective deathbeds. All of us were there to get some of that miraculous Anne Lamott juju on us. Not to overstate our collective adoration of the author, we were there to peek inside her inner Christ and rejoice.

Each time the heavy doors opened to allow in one or two of the chosen few, our hearts sank—if just for a moment. Will we get in to see her? Hear her? To touch her robes? Was the 169-mile drive from Detroit a waste of gas? In the end no one was turned away. There was, of course, room for everyone in Anne's house. We sat in communion to share the Anne experience—to laugh and cry and re-commit our faith to this imperfect world, to approach it bird by bird, to exhale and share our bananas.

Each in our own way, we found our inner Anne that afternoon—addict, mother, spiritual wanderer, citizen of the world, child of God. She read some of our favorites, her favorites and new a piece that warmed us all. She gave us the very personal gift of her pain for God's highest good.

Please Sign Here

After the crying and the laughing and the "ah ha" moments subsided, the moderator told those of us interested to wait patiently, because Anne herself would graciously be signing copies of her latest book. The queue began directly at the end of our pew. As God would have it, my BFF and I were first, albeit unprepared, in line. This was fortunate but awkward, as neither Sharon nor I had a book in hand.

Upon this realization, Sharon ran to the car where hers had been left behind. My situation was more of a dilemma. Truth be told, I'm not much of the "signing" type. I mean no disrespect to the mainstay of celebrity adoration, but I don't understand all the hoopla behind having a popular figure write his or her name on something I own, like a book or playbill or body part. Why would it matter if I had Kelsey Grammer's signature on a napkin? His name on a check—that I can use. I knew a guy—a designer of a popular '90s muscle car—who actually signed a woman's breast. What is the correct writing implement for that job?

Some celebrities seem offended when you don't ask for their autograph. Jay Leno pouted a bit when I denied him the thrill of writing his name in marker on a really big photo of his head. It wasn't that I didn't appreciate the offer, but really, I'm 50. The last time I cherished anything celebrity related was my 1976 Farrah Fawcett swimsuit poster. That iconic red swimsuit is now installed in the Smithsonian's National Museum of American History. Need I say more?

Anne's handlers quickly set up the makeshift office—folding banquet tables, opening cartons of books, setting up bottles of water and uncapping pens. I stood in line like a boob. No book. No BFF. Feeling foolish and excited and totally out of place, like at a junior-high dance. Finally, I got the signal to approach.

"OK, we're ready," the assistant pointed at me. "Come on in."

I did the fake look around, point to myself, "Oh, you mean me," thing people do when they're trying to be coy. Then I took a half-dozen baby steps forward.

Anne was sublime behind the desk. She was much smaller than I imagined based on her self-effacing descriptions. Her thighs did not at all look like "beloved old aunties," nor did her hair look like an octopus. She radiated kindness and peace, as if to say, "Here, sit, I have all day. Please have a cup of tea and tell me all about it." She was exactly the way I would expect a person to be if they really did do what Jesus did.

I'll admit, I was star struck. Frozen, dorky and without Sharon there to make everything okay, I did the first thing that came to mind: I dug into the fifth pocket of my jeans and pulled out my one-year sobriety token. Having no teleprompter or prepared remarks, I handed it to her across the table, hoping it would say the things I could not.

Anne took it and examined both sides. It was obviously familiar to her in a way only an addict could recognize. A smile spread across her face as if she had just found her favorite pen, or a house key she'd been searching for, but knew would eventually turn up.

"You helped me get sober," I said sheepishly.

By then she was already flying around the table—a cashmere whirling dervish. She took the token and kissed it and then kissed me and we embraced forever. Tears were streaming from my eyes.

164

"You were a kind of second sponsor to me," I managed to say. "I just kept reading. You gave me hope."

I can't remember what she said, something about proud and miraculous and God, but in a perfectly constructed Anne Lamott way that made me cry some more. We were in a wrinkle of time—a moment divined by God to share in the communion of healing. In the brilliance of her presence I felt the grace of God, this kind and loving God who was still new to me. In that moment I was baptized—my life choices were affirmed. I knew my feet were on the right path.

Clumsy and out-of-breath, Sharon bumped her way to the head of the line and joined us. I gave Anne the 20-second introduction—best friend, took me to rehab, introduced me to God, gave me your books, brought me here to celebrate my sobriety. Anne repeated the demonstration—the kissing and hugging and laughing and handing out joy. I was ready to pack her up and take the three of us home. The circle was complete.

Meanwhile, however, a couple hundred women with daggers for eyes were growing restless and annoyed at our mutual-admiration convention. They, too, wanted some Anne-ness. Anne signed a book for Sharon's daughter and we left the church on a cloud.

Message in a Bottle, But Not That Kind of Bottle

It's impossible to put into words an overarching moral to this story—to sum it up into a spiritual tag line.

I know it has something to do with giving and receiving, the St. Francis prayer, detachment, and the will of God—not necessarily in that order.

It was more than five years between those two events—the case of the kissing coins, as Nancy Drew might call them. But as unrelated as they were, I believe they were the exact same manifestation of trust. When Anne Lamott sat down to write about her experiences and eventually share her stories, she had no idea what would come of it. She opened her heart and let God do the rest. How could she know her words would comfort a strung-out closeted lesbian struggling to stay sober? How would she know her stories would resonate with me, assuage me, and help me feel a bit more connected to the planet? How could she know her pain, seasoned with laughter and a brutal dose of honesty would—on many nights—save me from picking up a drink?

She absolutely didn't. But she absolutely did.

"Wherever two or more of you are gathered in my name," God says in Matthew 18:20, "I am there."

Anne knew she'd find me and that I'd find her back. When you're doing God's will, that's how it works. Just like I found the Mother Teresa lady and she found me right back.

I believe there is no greater joy than to cast your bottle into the ocean, and know that someone, somewhere, will find God's message of hope inside.

TLL

Pray for a Pony

I was taught prayer in catechism somewhere between learning the many ways one could be damned to hell and the rules for softball. Our prayer was rote, like learning multiplication tables and state capitals. Like all mechanical learning, we avoided the messy business of delving into any underlying meaning. Who knew we were doing exactly what Jesus requested us not to some 2,000 years earlier when He said, "Use not vain repetitions, as the heathen do: for they think that they shall be heard for their much speaking." The whole time I kept repeating "Holy Mary Mother of God," I was really just wasting the Big Guy's time.

Many of my recovery friends recount the same experiences growing up. We laugh, for example, at our common misunderstandings of "The Lord's Prayer." How we thought God's real name was "Art" or that trespasses were the sins of cutting across your neighbor's front lawn. Was "temptation" really "Penn Station?" Would God deliver us from "weevils" or "Weebles?" And was it wrong to pray for ham and cheese to go with our daily bread? While it provided big laughs over coffee and donuts, our collective memories revealed just how clueless we were in our petitions to God.

I was taught a number of prayers in catechism, drilled on them weekly, and told my very soul depended upon me knowing them backward and forward. Even at gunpoint, I couldn't remember a single one today. Funny, I also don't remember the state capital of New Hampshire.

My Aunt Mary Ester, a woman who curiously neither married nor became a nun, recited the marathon of all prayers, "The Rosary," every night before bed. I thought she was "speaking in tongues"—whatever that meant. I remember falling asleep to a murmur of grief seeping out from under her bedroom door whenever I had the misfortune of spending the night at her house. Hers was a type of wailing whisper, a trance-like narrative of mystical pain. I was certain this verbal suffering would one day be required of me—added to the repertoire of empty words I had to memorize and regurgitate to be considered worthy by God.

My aunt called her nightly prayer ritual "working the Rosary," as if she was disinfecting the toilet bowl or balancing her checkbook. Since when is communicating with God "work?" I guess when the prayer has more verses than, "1,000 Bottles of Beer on the Wall."

Here's my take on the Rosary: Any religious practice that begins with a string of beads doused in perfumed oil, milk, melted butter or any other anointed fluid leaves me skeptical. Really, if you need an abacus to keep track of your prayer, there's probably something fishy about it. There's even a "Prayer after the Rosary Prayer," which contains deleted scenes, director's notes and hilarious outtakes. A devotional obstacle course more complicated than three-handed bridge does not bring me closer to God.

Required prayer was just another part of my family's religious pretense. Conveniently, it was also used as punishment. As penance for my bad behavior and unholy thoughts, I was instructed to pray. The worse my crime, the more prayers I'd be made to recite. Eventually I began lying in Confession to avoid the Virgin Mary, Fatima, and the whole cast of Biblical characters with freakishly long names like Bashanhavothjair and Mahershalalhashbaz. To me, prayer was on par with being grounded, losing my dessert privileges and all access to network programming. How was I to understand that these prayers were actually my link to God?

Prayer in a Nut Shell

My best friend, years before I got sober, tried to engage me in prayer. She was praying mightily for my drunken ass and recruited me to join her. Lord knows it was at least a two-man job. She even dumbed it down to my level. She knew the heavy handed approach—"open your Bible to page 534"—wouldn't fly, so she gave me an article from a popular women's magazine to guide me through the prayer process. This type of magazine is

169

best known for solving the world's problems—bad bosses, unruly hair, cheating husbands, cellulite—in 500 words or less. This article was aptly titled, "How to Pray." Since I was still drinking, I never read word one.

I'll let you in on a little secret: You can't pray stoned. You can, but all the prayers come out:

- "Please Lord, don't let that cop in my rear-view mirror pull me over."
- "God, if you get me out of this mess I'll never drink again."
- "Jesus, don't let my husband find out."
- "Christ, where's the vodka?"

These aren't real prayers, they're bunker prayers. They are the kind of prayers one might say hiding in a shelter in Afghanistan with an atomic missile locked on your ass with no chance in hell of getting out. Not unlike being an active alcoholic.

Monkey See, Monkey Pray

Once I got sober I began in earnest to learn how to pray, if for no other reason than to fit in. Everyone in recovery was bragging about their morning and evening prayer, as if they had swum the English Channel or eaten a dozen Habanero peppers. It seemed to be working for them and I wanted to be part of the club.

Like everything else in early sobriety, I needed to keep prayer simple. I actually found that prayer-lite article handed to me by my friend years earlier. That imbecilic "How to Pray" story was exactly what I needed. It told me that it didn't matter who or what I prayed to, or my choice of words, the direction I faced, what I did with my hands or how long to wait after a meal. The point was I just needed to muster enough willingness to try. I didn't even need to believe in what I was doing. All I needed was the willingness to take that first step.

Willingness has never been my strong suit, nor does it run in my family. We are stubborn—German on my mother's side and just plain donkey on my dad's. My Oma would stare at me across the kitchen table challenging me to try some of her German cooking—the really bad stuff like offal and sauerkraut surprise—while I sat at the other end, mouth pinned shut in defiance. No way was that crap passing through my lips. At the age of eight, I had no willingness to become a connoisseur of world cuisine.

Willingness for me—as for most alcoholics—comes when I run out of options and when there's nothing left to risk (or eat). When the pain gets great enough, willingness is often right around the corner. That's when I started to pray. I was exhausted and defeated, the latter being the perfect criterion for willingness. Defeat is great motivation for trying lots of crazy shit. I guess if my grandmother had ever run out of chocolate crinkle cookies, I would eventually have eaten the Schweinshaxe (pig knuckles).

Today willingness is the foundation of my relationship with God. It is my first prayer of the day:

"God please keep me coming back to You, give me the willingness to seek Your strength and guidance." If I pray for willingness I know I'm practicing humility and I'm becoming teachable. Two very good things.

Our Tiger, Who Art in a Rehab Facility for Sex Addiction

My second prayer breakthrough came from an equally questionable source, a sliver of a book entitled *The Prayer of Jesus* by Hank Hanegraaff. I found the book tucked on a shelf at the house of the same best friend. I figured if the author was good enough to be among her trusted spiritual advisors, I would give him a read.

The problem: Hanegraaff used golf tediously throughout his writing as a parable for life, prayer and his relationship with God. He couldn't have used football or sex or puppies or any number of things I really like as his literary device. No, it had to be golf.

It was miraculous I didn't toss this book into the nearest sand trap. It was "Tiger Woods" this and "Tiger Woods" that. It was written at a time when the golfer himself was a symbol for Christ.

Putting the putting and driving and chipping aside, I found the book insightful with actual tools I could use to improve my prayer relationship with God. My favorite is Hank's easy-to-use acronym: F-A-C-T-S, which stands for **F**aith, **A**doration, **C**onfession, **T**hanksgiving and

Supplication. It's so simple even a child can use it and that's why it works for me.

I use Hank's suggestion daily to center myself for prayer. I focus on an individual letter for a moment, concentrating on what each word represents to me that day. For example: Faith means hope and belief; Adoration means praise and glory; Confession means transparency and forgiveness; Thanksgiving means grace and gratitude; Supplication means "Knock and the door shall be answered."

Prayer is a way to reaffirm my love of God, not—as Hank reminds me—God's customer service window for my endless demands and complaints. I tend to communicate with God like Santa, starting and ending with, "I want, I want, I want." And then, "I want some more."

Hank writes, "Prayer is not a magic formula to get things from God. Communicating with God in prayer is itself the prize, a means of pursuing a relationship with our heavenly Father."

I often still like a gumball at the end.

The Prayer That Jesus Prayed

I've been blessed on my spiritual journey with people who've shared their favorite prayers and devotionals. I've collected them over the years like treasured shells. Always on my mind is Emmet Fox's deconstruction of "The Lord's Prayer," from his "Sermon on the Mount."

173

He took the prayer that confounded me and gave it purpose.

From author, Anne Lamott, I received what she describes as the only two prayers needed in communicating with God: "Help me, help me, help me," and "Thank you, thank you, thank you." As she says, "There's hardly an excuse for not remembering the words."

Rounding out my short list of top prayers is the "Third Step Prayer" of Alcoholics Anonymous, the "Serenity Prayer," the "Prayer of St. Francis," and—while not official prayers, I love Philippians 4:13: "I can do all things through Christ who strengthens me," and Psalm 46:10: "Be still and know that I am God."

While these are all fabulous platforms to jump start me into communion with my higher power, prayer for me is an individual expression. It's personal. The prefabricated scripts written hundreds of years ago by councils of morose white guys in musty monasteries don't quite fit me—like skinny jeans. My conversations with God need to reflect the ever evolving, ever discovering, ever teetering on the edge—me. While I'm sure the "Novenas to Annunciation" is a beautiful and uplifting devotion, it usually doesn't capture the moment.

This morning's moment was spent accompanying my dear, sweet 83 year old neighbor to the orthopedic surgeon. She's been complaining of shoulder pain for months, and physical therapy and cortisone shots have provided her no relief. She wants an operation. I think that's the stupidest idea I've ever heard. I say unless you're lying in the road with no pulse and bleeding from your eyeballs, hospitals are no place for people, especially the elderly. But that's my opinion, which isn't worth shit, and if expressed will likely start World War Three. So my very spontaneous prayer this morning went something like this:

"Good morning, God. Thanks for a good night's sleep. Thanks for listening and always being on-call. As you know, I'm taking Agnes to the doctor today. I'm asking you get on board with this. Please help me keep my pie-hole shut and allow me to be an instrument of your love. Help me comfort Agnes through your strength and guidance. Whatever the outcome, I'd really appreciate it if we could get through this with minimal frustration and name calling. If you can join us in the exam room, I'd consider it a personal favor. It might take a while; I suggest bringing a good book. Please know I am trying to be part of the solution although my behavior might reflect otherwise. Thank you for giving me the willingness to seek your way. I love you. I'll check in with you throughout the day. Thanks. PS –I'd appreciate a close parking space if one is available."

There's no way my third grade catechism teacher could have prepared me with that prayer. And I'm sure you won't find it in any Christian-approved literature. It's just the "Prayer of Charlotte, 8:23 a.m." I speak to

God with reverence, but let's not kid ourselves. He won't be surprised by an occasional F-bomb or my improper punctuation. He's God, not an Ivy League rhetoric professor.

Stop, Drop and Pray

It's not an exaggeration to say I pray all the time now. I try to stay in constant contact with my higher power throughout the day. I force people to sit in silence while I pray before meals. I pray at recovery meetings and especially in the car. I've been known to pray during particularly difficult conversations with my partner. And not just, "Dear God, I wish she'd shut up!" If I keep the pipeline open, I figure I can't stray too far from God's voice.

Early in recovery, I had a job coordinating a new car launch in Monterey and things were definitely not going my way. Too many boozy and demanding auto executives, bad road tires, too little help, a decrepit racetrack—the whole thing was making me crazy. At the first opportunity, I ducked into a hotel elevator and dropped to my knees. Prayer seems to work best for me in that position. I calculated I had 12 floors to connect with God and get my head out of my ass. Imagine my surprise when the elevator stopped on the third floor, and a well-dressed couple toting sports drinks and tennis rackets got in. I hadn't expected company during my private prayer vigil, not even those going to the roof-top courts. From the looks on their faces, neither did Biff or Buffy. I pretended to look for a nonexistent contact lens for the next nine floors and then returned to my conversation with God for the ride down.

Short Attention Span Theatre

Never allowing a film to form on my spiritual pudding, my therapist Diane is now prodding me to take prayer to the "next level." I reminded her that even God rested on the seventh day. She's introduced a mysterious 10-letter word into my vocabulary—meditation. "What's next," I mocked, "Kool-Aid drinking, head shaving, tambourine rattling?"

I've often heard that prayer is talking to God, and meditation is listening. Listen? To God? Wow, I missed that memo. I usually just spew off my agenda, expect God to take care of it, and go on with my very important business—like napping. I didn't know there was a "Part B."

I remember my first-grade teacher Mrs. Stevens—when it was still permissible to invoke the name of our Creator in public school—telling me God made us with two ears and one mouth so that we'd listen twice as much as we spoke. Nice try. While it's true that I have only one mouth, it's super big. It takes up most of my face.

No one I know—except Diane—does meditation very well. She meditates perfectly, often using "The Lord's Prayer" and incorporating exercise at the same time. It's

177

enough to make me gag. I can't even meditate while meditating.

As she power-walks her 10-mile course (and no doubt rescues kittens from burning buildings along the way), she selects a word or phrase from that prayer—or another—as a meditative starter pistol. She may pick (for example) "our"—the first word of the prayer—as her touchstone for the day. Here's what it might sound like inside her well-coiffed head:

"Our" means belonging to us; of us; in our family. What does it mean to be in a family? My family? God's family? "Our" establishes the relationship between man and God, of father and son, made in God's image. What is God's image? How am I like God? Do we all share the power of God? Why do I sometimes feel apart from God? Do I see God in all people? Do I recognize the inner-dwelling Christ in me? What responsibilities do I have as a child of God? How do I understand the wholeness of the world, our connectedness and how we are all one?"

This unscripted "Q&A" with God is her way of drawing deeper into communion with Him. She ponders each of these thoughts—listening for God's voice throughout the day. I've tried to practice this technique while jogging, mirroring her introspective approach. It usually comes out, "God, I'm dying. Please let me get hit by a UPS truck."

But I Really Want a Pony

My best friend and I regularly discuss spirituality, God's will, religion and the Bible. It isn't how you'd imagine it—we don't meet in her kitchen over hot tea and lemon squares wearing flowered aprons. Our conversations are about real life, which is often raw and ugly and painful. We're usually on the phone, on the fly and out of our minds. I'll blurt out a question like, "How do you know if you're doing God's will," and we're off to the races.

Our favorite topic—on which we disagree—continues to be, "How to Pray?" Her position is God welcomes prayers involving specific requests, like a DJ at a wedding reception. She believes wholeheartedly that it's perfectly okay to pray for a pony. That's our shorthand for praying for a particular outcome—something you really want. If you have your heart set on a pony, she argues, by all means pray for a pony. I, on the other hand, am less direct, less demanding and infinitely more fearful. I pray only for God's will, knowing it might not result in anything remotely equine. Since I don't have a clue what's best for me, I believe it's best to give that job to God.

Here's an example: The BFF's academically gifted daughter recently applied to a prestigious private school. In addition to discussing the financing, carpooling, and our bitterness that at the tender age of 14, she's about to blow us out of the water at *Jeopardy!*, we considered the appropriate request to place before God.

"I'm going to pray she gets admitted," the proud mother exclaimed. "What's wrong with that? Why wouldn't God want Claire to go to Elitist Academy?"

"That's the whole point," I said, beaming with spiritual superiority. "We don't know God's will. Perhaps He has another plan for her. Maybe we should just pray for God to give Claire the strength to accept any outcome."

"That's stupid," she defended. "The whole point of supplication is putting our requests in front of God and asking for His help."

"Maybe we're just arguing semantics," I said. "But I'll tell you, if I had received all the things I prayed for over the years, I'd have been royally fucked."

"May I remind you that YOU WERE!" she responded.

It's tough to dispute the facts.

As a postscript to the story, the BFF prayed for her daughter's admission into the school, where Claire became a star pupil. Which just proves, what the hell do I know?

Just Like a Prayer, but Not an Actual Prayer

Doesn't—sometimes—God just want us to have the pony? I mean, He isn't sitting in heaven trying to foil my dreams and make my life miserable. I can do a good job of that all by myself.

I just can't see God saying, "Little Timmy just keeps praying for that damn pony, selfish rat bastard. I guess I'll just have to give him cholera instead. Might have to lay his dad off from work, too."

Even if you've evolved to the top of the spiritual food chain, you can't convince me that sometimes it wouldn't be nice to pray for a specific outcome—for the shoulder operation to work out well or to reconcile with your mother or for a close friend to beat a disease.

But instead of the pony, I'm counseled to stick to the prayer that—according to Emmet Fox—never fails: "Thy will be done."

That's just it. I don't know God's will. All I have is my plan, built on ego and arrogance and the pursuit of pleasure. I didn't say it was a good plan.

Let Us Pray

Lately I've been asking Diane for prayer suggestions and for the perfect script to petition God.

"Pray for willingness, strength and guidance," she said. "For God's blessing. For the brotherhood of man. Ask God to hold us all up in love for His highest good. Pray for the power to do His will. Ask God to make you an instrument of His peace."

Her best and most adamant advice, however, is to stop worrying about the words. After all, she says, "He knows what things you need before you ask him." According to Diane, He also knows when I've been sleeping, awake, bad or good. She's forever encouraging me to be, "Good, for goodness sake!"

A Steaming Heap of Grace

Before bed, I hit my knees to acknowledge and thank God for all of my blessings. I then reflect on my behavior and ask myself, "How well did I serve God today?" It's at that moment I am reminded that it is our deeds—and not our words—that truly matter.

"It is our lives that are our prayers," Diane says. "Not what comes from our mouths. Living in harmony with God's will, bringing forth the Kingdom of Heaven, practicing love and forgiveness above all things. That is communicating with God. That is the living prayer."

"And," she said with a bit of a grin, "if you really need to pray for the pony, you better pray it comes with a big shovel. You're going to need it."

TLL

Secrets

To the women at our weekly 12-step recovery group, Abby confessed she had started drinking again.

"It's really not that bad," she urged us to believe. "Just vodka in the basement after my husband and the baby are asleep. I'm not hurting anyone. I just don't feel I have any other choices."

Lord knows how long she had kept that a secret.

This Part is the Flashback

In the fall of 1982, I returned to Michigan State to begin my sophomore year. I would be living with Robin—the love of my life—who was just beginning her collegiate career. Robin and I met in high school, fell obsessively in love and began a closeted lesbian relationship. To call it closeted would be an understatement. We were in the closet, behind an unmarked panel that hid a set of stairs, which led to a vacant room that existed in an alternative universe.

The day we moved into the dorm, we celebrated by screwing three brand new locks into the door that opened (through a shared bathroom) into the adjoining suite. Our secret would remain our secret. We got high and were about to get down to some serious sex when we were interrupted by a forceful knock on the freshly bolted door. The thing about dope—or should I say one of the things about dope—is that the smell will not be denied. It's not like we were in our room hanging curtains or off at the campus bookstore buying spiral notebooks and matching highlighters. We were in our room and we were busted. I put my clothes back on and opened the door just enough for a bit of smoke to crawl through.

The person on the other side would change my life in ways I did not know possible.

"Whatcha doing?" said a sing-song voice that came from an exploding head of hair.

"We're just, um, (cough) hanging out," I said, snickering, not intending it as an invitation.

"Great!"

The body connected to the hair pushed her way in and plopped down on the pull-out couch as if she'd been doing it for 20 years.

So it began. I had just met my Sundance Kid, my Han Solo, my Thelma.

Her name was Abby Chesney. She was from Delaware and—coming from Riverview, Michigan—a place I thought wildly exotic. By that evening, we were cemented in friendship. Had we been children living along the Mississippi Delta in 1897, we'd have bloodied our fingers and become kin.

Our friendship would more aptly have been described as a spree—reckless, and in our minds, legendary. We were not bad in the traditional sense—we didn't hold up

184

liquor stores or push old people into oncoming traffic. But with Abby, everything was an adventure, a caper, a prank.

We rarely went to class, rarely were sober, rarely took showers (maybe that was just me) and rarely suffered any consequences. The two of us differed only in that I was monogamous, remaining faithful to Robin throughout our arduous relationship.

Abby had a different story. Come morning, you'd never know who you'd meet in our shared bathroom. Maybe hers was normal freshman behavior. But to me, it seemed like a lot of men.

Risky Business

After a few months in our closely confined dormitory, I wanted to come out to Abby. It was exhausting for Robin and me to keep our tracks covered. To my surprise, Robin agreed, and in what was the riskiest move of my young 19 years, we told Abby we were a couple. An amazing thing happened. Abby didn't walk away in disgust or hurl ugly remarks. Instead, she told me she loved me and that it didn't matter. She agreed to keep our secret.

Our bond was tight, but not healthy. We were accomplices to each other's undoing, co-authoring our stories of shame. She would not judge my sexual orientation, and I would not judge her sexual promiscuity. I lived in the eerie shadow of society's judgment; she thrived on attention, finding it nightly and briefly. In the end, we both just desperately wanted to be loved.

It wasn't long before Abby got pregnant. While Robin and I were told it was unplanned, I don't think anyone in the U.S. older than 14 gets pregnant accidentally. The statistical failure rate for condoms is between 1.6 and 3.6 percent. I'm gay and even I know how reproduction works.

Abby was in the process of flunking out of school anyway, so her return to Delaware was not unexpected. She had the baby, and for the next three years yo-yo'd between raising her son there and trying to make a family with the baby's father in Michigan. She even lived in an apartment with me after my graduation—not the ideal environment to raise a little boy. It was a difficult time, filled with personal destruction.

Abby's relationship with the boy's father culminated in a nasty custody battle over their son. It was a smart decision to split, but resulted in the messiness of lawyers and judges and courtrooms.

I was subpoenaed by the baby's father to impeach Abby's character. No one knew better the insanity of Abby's lifestyle—one that would not have her winning any "Mother of the Year" awards. Under oath, I would have to testify to the drinking, the drugs, her indiscriminant sex and the other reckless behavior in which we were both engaged.

The day after I received my directive to appear in court from Mr. Baby-Daddy, I received a call from

Abby's lawyer. Abby had told her attorney about my secret life and they threatened to use it to Abby's advantage.

I was given an ultimatum: Lie under oath about Abby's lifestyle or they'd reveal I was a lesbian.

It was my secret or hers.

I did not ask to be part of Abby's *Kramer vs Kramer*. I had my own crumbling world to deal with. Robin was trying to break free of me and had, without my knowledge, begun dating the man who would eventually become her husband. I was trying to string together a career from part-time jobs that would allow me to stay in Lansing—away from the judgment of my parents and small-minded hometown.

In a surprising turn of events, the two parties settled out of court at the 11th hour. I never did take the stand. Nor did I intend to ever see Abby again. My secret was to remain with me, like a cancer, till my end.

Today I'm familiar with the phrase, "Our secrets keep us sick." I was not in 1985. So as I watched my life unravel, I kept it all inside. Every secret, every ounce of shame and betrayal and abandonment stayed under lock and key inside me. Killing me not so softly over time.

Nothing Happens by Mistake

Fast forward some 20-odd years to an early morning 12-step meeting where I'm nearly three years sober. As I work to stay awake, my eyes wander around the church's fellowship hall and fix on one very loud person with an east-coast accent and beautifully bushy hair. I do a double take, a triple take and an indefensible stare. I ask the woman sitting next to me if she knows the crazy-haired woman at the far table.

"Sure," she said. "That's Abby."

Some people call such remarkable situations coincidences; I choose to call them God-incidences.

Perhaps I had a panic attack, perhaps it was the Pad-Thai from the night before, but I leapt for the bathroom. Here was the woman who'd been dead to me for two decades—someone who at one time was my other half. She was now sitting 20 feet from me, testifying the same way all alcoholics do.

I approached her after the meeting. It was, as the saying goes, as if no time had passed. We fell back together fast and hard. I was there immediately after the birth of her second child. I envied her—married, with children, money and long-term sobriety. She had much of what I thought I wanted, but with slightly different packaging.

Not too long after our reconciliation, Abby relapsed.

In life, there are no guarantees.

Taking it to My Grave

No one knows the reason for Abby's relapse, except maybe Abby. I could guess—marriage and money, job stress and the baby. But the real reason is buried down deep. The real reason lies in a secret.

Before I got sober I told my therapist I drank because I was gay. I tried to convince her that my life was too difficult and ugly to face without a crutch. She reminded me that not all homosexuals are alcoholic. She wasn't letting me off the hook that easy.

After years of digging, of building trust and tearing down walls, I was finally able to say my secret: I believe I am unlovable. All that crap about being a lesbian and judgmental parents and wanting to be normal was just that—crap. With my secret uncovered, I could begin to deal—with the drugs and alcohol, my family of origin, the desire to be loved, the self-loathing and the fear of dying alone. Had I not unleashed my secret, it would become my prophecy.

No secret can harm me if I don't keep it a secret.

Not Three Mile Island

Not long ago I met a childhood friend of my partner. Within the first hour of meeting this woman, I knew more about her than some of my own best friends. And not just where she worked or whether she preferred Coke or Pepsi. I'm talking about the stuff that makes you blush and even squirm a little in your seat. While I'm no poster child for disclosure—I'd known my best friend for more than a decade before I told her I was gay—Sharon's friend set a new standard for TMI.

I was at first aghast. Did I really want to know about the noisy sex with her husband? The contagious skin disease caused by dirty hotel sheets? The last time she messed her pants?

What would Miss Manners call a woman who discussed—with a total stranger—her husband's genitals, the family's deteriorating finances, her affinity for pain medication and the continuing saga of Rover's erratic bowels?

Totally inappropriate, I'd guess.

But what the hell does Miss Manners know?

After a few hours pondering this woman's naked admissions, I changed my mind, as I so often do.

Maybe she wasn't just nuts. Maybe her unflappable transparency was a message from God.

"Pay attention," said God in her usual Carol Burnett voice. "There's going to be a test on this."

What Would Jesus Hide?

What would life be like—what would the world be like—if we no longer kept secrets?

If we all spoke our truth and sang our song and showed our underpants a little?

What if we felt safe to share the things we hide, say the words we fear and speak without shame?

What if we were free to say:
- I ate the ten bags of candy I bought for Halloween;
- My boobs are now lower than my navel;
- I only clean my house before my in-laws visit;
- I watched 42 episodes of *General Hospital* instead of reading *Moby Dick* for book club;

- I wish I hadn't smoked dope in high school and gotten expelled;
- We can't have children;
- My husband sometimes hits me when he's been drinking;
- We can't pay the IRS;
- I'm not a very good mother;
- I drive drunk.

After Dinner Mint

Secrets are like live hand grenades. If you hold them too long—Kaboom!

I would have taken my secrets to my grave. And almost did.

Now I try to live my life without secrets. If I feel the need to keep something hidden, there's usually a pretty bad reason why. If I live my life in the open I can't hurt me, and neither can anyone else.

I have a suggestion: After you take your lesbian to lunch, tell her one of your secrets.

There. It's out.

No more reason to hide.

No more guilt or shame.

The secret has no power.

Do you feel 20-pounds lighter?

Good, now you have room for dessert.

TLL

191

Hear That Voice Again

A young man new in recovery was eager to share his ongoing spiritual quest.

"I've searched everywhere," he told an old timer. "Christianity, Eastern religion, fasts, cults, philosophy, mysticism ... even drumming—all trying to find God."

"Looking for God?" the old man questioned and shook his head. "He ain't lost."

* * *

Even when my dad passed away, I couldn't muster the enthusiasm to attend mass. Enthusiasm is—of course—the wrong sentiment. I can't quite describe my church antipathy. Maybe it was a lack of willingness, a fear of the past or a sense of hypocrisy. Whatever the case, I grieved for my father in my own time and space—mostly on my therapist's couch.

My church going has—for the past 12-plus years—been relegated to the basements and fellowship halls where recovery meetings are held. I rarely find myself in the sanctuaries reserved for religious worship. I'm like my grandmother that way. She passed her days in churches—but playing pinochle with like-minded octogenarians—not singing from hymnals or quoting scripture. She believed the maintenance of her spirituality was exclusively between her and God in a rather free-range format.

Church has not been my classroom of spiritual enlightenment. Since childhood, I've found church foreboding—too many depictions of a tortured Christ, too many people proclaiming to be God's mouthpiece, too many rules that seemed counterintuitive to God's love of us.

As a child, I was forced against my will to sit sandwiched between my mom and dad, and not allowed to peep for 60 minutes—a near impossibility for me. Swatting your kid just because she dozes off during the homily—is that really the way God rolls?

After a half century, I can say with certainty that within the confines of the Catholic Church, God and I never made a love connection.

It's Christmas, Charlie Brown

I've not wept for my churchless self, nor am I spiritually adrift. Today, God and I are—in a word— good. In a kind of born free, neo-spiritual, make-it-up-as-you-go, Old Country Buffet kind of way. It's working for me. I believe the feeling is mutual.

So you can imagine the surprise I had last December upon hearing a small voice inside me whisper an odd request. It wasn't the usual demand for salty snacks or sex or an afternoon nap. My little voice said it wanted to attend Midnight Mass.

A traditional church service, it said. One with a nativity scene, the Eucharist and "Angels We Have Heard on High." The voice wanted it all—a proper outfit, a proper offering and a proper attitude. My spiritual world was rocked.

The calendar read Dec. 20. Perhaps I had heard the voice incorrectly. Perhaps instead of "Midnight Mass" the voice said, "Midnight Madness," as in late night, pre-Christmas super sales. In response, I rushed my partner to J.C. Penny at 11:15 p.m. to satisfy the voice with shopping bags filled with deeply discounted holiday merchandise.

But the voice would not be fooled. "Midnight Mass," it demanded; the time-honored tradition of a Christmas Eve church service. Little did I know what my voice had in mind.

Do You Hear What I Hear?

I often wonder about the voice inside me, the voice that directs my actions and non-actions. I actually have several voices that speak to me: I'm bombarded with competing personalities, some of whom are manic and highly caffeinated. The good news: I'm beginning to discern the harmful voices from those inspired by God. It might sound obvious, but hearing God's voice isn't always easy. Sometimes I think I hear the Holy Spirit at Target, telling me to fill my cart with essential family-sized toiletries and decorative throw pillows. Then I remember God is not an in-store circular. I look forward to the day God's voice becomes second nature to me, like breathing out and breathing in. Until then, I have to be constantly vigilant of who's using my internal intercom. It's amazing how much the Lord can sound like Homer Simpson.

I hear God when I am still and quiet. Unfortunately, I'm rarely in that state. But if I slow my mind and breathe, I can hear God over the panic-driven addict who runs on fear. Yes, despite my many attempts to break up with her, she's still in the picture.

Like a Christmas Carol

Like a big, fat, annoying squirrel, the voice had built a nest in my head. So I sat and waited and prayed for God's love to wash over me.

"Remember the Christ in Christmas," the voice said. "For just an hour, join the choir of angels."

I followed the voice.

And I'm so glad I did. For it brought me to love God in three new and magical ways.

Just Google God

When I told my partner I would be attending mass late on Dec. 24, she gave me that, "Did you have a closed-head injury while I was away at work" look she reserves for my more curious behaviors. It's a look she has perfected and uses with surprising frequency. After attempting to explain the "little voice" with limited success, she merely said in a monotone voice, "I shall come with you." My partner, God bless her, accompanies me on many of my spiritual treasure hunts without judgment. I really like that about her.

Finding a church service these days is as easy as finding a local movie. Not easy for me personally, but for others with smart devices and things called "apps." One such electronic wizard is my new friend Mark. He was at our house early Christmas Eve attending the 10:00 a.m. recovery meeting we host every year.

"I want to attend mass tonight," I asked him in a hushed voice. "Can you please help me find a service?"

"Sure," he said, wrangling his Droid from his low-slung jeans.

Within minutes, Mark had amassed a long list of times, driving directions and "posts" for religious services within a five-mile radius of our house. I guess anyone with a data plan could have done the same. The bonus was Mark's personalized input. Within seconds, he provided a first-hand evaluation of the many churches—their quality of service, ministers, congregations, running time and gay friendly (or unfriendly) vibe. Mark was indeed better than Moviefone.

Why did my 24-year-old recovery friend have a trove of religious intelligence at his ready? One piece of information I forgot to mention about my young pal: Mark is training to become a priest.

Follow the (Rock) Star

The first time I met Mark he was barely sober—a week or two at best. He staggered into a recovery meeting held in a church basement not a mile from my house. It was, coincidentally, the same meeting I first staggered into more than twelve years ago when I entered the program.

Mark is a combination John the Baptist, Kid Rock and Gene Kelly. Not that he's much of a dancer that I know of, but Mark is an old soul in a Christian's body who can party like a rock star. He is gentle and senior beyond his years (his drink of choice was a Rob Roy) but with an obvious background in debauchery. He is a graduate of one of Michigan's public institutions of higher education and a disciple of Delta Tau Chi fraternity. Mark has the entire urban dictionary committed to memory, along with most of the Bible. He is part of my growing body of spiritual peeps breaking the mold of traditional Jesus followers.

Mark directed me to St. John's Episcopal Church for its 10:30 p.m. mass—the closest thing to midnight we could find. I had, coincidentally, spent many hours in that very church's clammy basement, drinking muddy recovery coffee and praying for my addiction to be lifted. Now it was time to join the "normal people" on the main level of God's house, the ones who are prompt, know all of the songs by heart and can tell you the exact location of the bathrooms.

I had promised my little voice one hour and I was about to make good on that promise. Based on my Catholic upbringing, my partner and I arrived roughly 90 minutes before the service was scheduled to begin. When we arrived, the parking lot of St. John's Episcopal Church was empty. The church was dark. Who were these Episcopals, anyway?

I immediately sent Mark a text.

"U R 2 early," he replied. Apparently.

Killing time, Sharon and I left to purchase hot holiday drinks and tour the local neighborhood, looking at Christmas lights. We sang along with Karen Carpenter. We pointed out dogs in argyle sweaters. We laughed at tacky decorations, agreeing camels and Frosty don't belong in the same holiday tableau.

The lot was still vacant when we returned. We waited in silence. One by one, smart, energy-efficient sedans and compact crossovers filled the empty spaces. And lots of Subarus.

Like animals boarding the ark—or maybe a gay Carnival cruise ship, women—two-by-two and arm-in-arm—began a steady stream into the church's side door. I said a quick prayer, took a few deep breaths and with my partner joined the flight of odd birds twisting down halls past classrooms and offices. We arrived at the sanctuary, where we were welcomed warmly, given individual candles with cardboard bibs and handed little playbooks to help first timers like us understand the run of the show and principle players.

198

The church was beautiful, decked in aromatic cedar and pine, and wrapped like a package in bows and lights. To the left of the alter sat a mixed adult choir and instrumental ensemble. Like Goldilocks, we moved our seats several times until we found a place we felt comfortable—not too close to the front or anyone else—just a nondescript location with a great view.

The look and smell of the church conjured a feeling of familiarity, but nothing was quite familiar. This was a house I knew, but a place I'd never been.

The Supporting Cast

Not everyone in church that evening looked like Janet Reno, but more did than not. Maybe it was the chopped gray hair, the abundance of men's shoes, or the John Wayne swagger during the Passing of the Peace. It was like a Snap-On tool convention for Christian women. Every girl's former gym teacher was sitting in those pews.

There were Hilary Clinton pant suits and Christmas sweaters adorned with working bells and bulbs. There were butches and femmes and women less gender conclusive. They were a blend of Annie Hall and Monty Hall, literally wearing their homosexuality on their sleeves. There was so much synthetic material I feared the entire congregation would burst into flames. But I always worry about that when I see gays in church.

A Midnight Mass filled with lesbians? Was it coincidence or God-incidence? The latter, I'm sure. I had

199

to laugh at the irony of God's message to me that night. Here I feared entering the house of God—the exclusive dwelling of breeding heterosexuals—and instead I found Home Depot on a Saturday night. There were, of course, a handful of obligatory straight couples with toddlers, moms with well-groomed sons, and moms with sons and their male "companions." But I couldn't get past the abundance of lesbians. Even the service was conducted by a lesbian, in lesbian, and with lesbians attending to the collateral chores usually delegated to 85 year old men wearing nametags and orthopedic shoes.

I was once again overjoyed at my ignorance, glad to be free of yet another misconception about my higher power. Of course His house would have many rooms and it would be welcome to all—Billie Jean King and Gertrude Stein and Jane Addams and me.

I thank God for these gals. They broke the glass ceiling of the lesbian world, having taken the slings and arrows of discrimination to make way for the rest of us. They lived closeted in fear of losing jobs, friends and family, and ultimately their lives. Those gals did what I might not have had the compunction to do, so that I can do what I'm free to do today. Which was largely the same thing we were all doing—listening to our little voice. We were looking in the strangely familiar cathedrals of our youth for a connection, or perhaps reconnection, with the One who never stopped loving us.

I said a prayer of gratitude for the socially awkward and poorly dressed congregation. They paved my path, not unlike Bill W. I owe them much—honor and respect, and the duty to be myself, hopefully making a difference for those who follow.

Mark 2.0

My next magical God moment came right after the New Year. My pal Mark invited me to a ceremony in his honor, marking a significant milestone in his spiritual pilgrimage—something to do with robes and staffs and the possibility of refreshments. Mark had been cast by God with a recurring cameo in my spiritual miniseries.

On that day Mark was being received as a Novice Brother into the Anamchara Fellowship—a monastic community committed to prayer and service. The moment was all Mark's—to shine in the glory of God and wear a cute little outfit that made him look like Friar Tuck. The whole thing reminded me of an ABC After-School Special starring Kirk Cameron.

She Might Have Been k.d. lang

The ceremony for Mark was conducted by a lovely woman named Gretchen, an official of the church in some capacity, who'd flown in from Anamchara headquarters in New Jersey to make the occasion legit.

Need I mention her sexual orientation?

Of course not.

There, preaching from the pulpit, offering Communion and speaking of love and inclusion, was

201

God's messenger to me. She was an overweight, middle-aged woman in Tevas wearing a green tablecloth on her head and inviting us all to eat from God's table. My God messenger was flabby and loud and radiating God's love like a nuclear power plant.

And I loved it.

Don't get me wrong—God's message had nothing whatsoever to do with lesbians.

No, God's message to me that day was, "Charlotte, it's time for you to know Me."

He was right. I'd never known my God. Just someone else's.

Will the Real God Please Stand Up?

When I first came into recovery, I was told I could create a higher power—"A god of my own understanding." While I was skeptical about inventing a new deity, I found the opportunity promising. The God of my then understanding—my dad's God—wasn't a particularly nice guy. The idea of a new-and-improved fun-sized God was intriguing.

People all around me were reinventing God—my sponsor, my therapist and the lesbians at St. John's. Gretchen was doing it with aplomb. This God was love and acceptance and service—a trinity of hope. Mark and his Evangelical buddies were devoting themselves to a God without boundaries.

These people were *getting* God. Who He was and what He was, and how He wanted us to be.

202

As I watched Gretchen welcome Mark into the Anamchara fellowship, I thanked my little voice. I was getting to see God—His myriad of shapes and sizes, colors and voices, with as many wardrobe changes as Lady Gaga.

I believe few of us in life are given a clean slate—a chance to shake the spiritual Etch-A-Sketch—and here, thanks to Mark, I'd been given two. I could reinvent me, and I could reinvent God.

God, Holding on Line Three

As much as it surprised me to meet Jesus on the Mackinac Bridge, I was equally startled to bump into Him at the Detroit Institute of Arts. I pegged Him as more of a Vatican Museum kind of guy.

The much heralded "Rembrandt and the Face of Jesus" exhibit came to the DIA around the time Mark took his vows. Everyone I knew crowed about it, reviewers touted it—apparently appealing to believers and non-believers alike. Even my little voice whispered excitedly about it.

For the record, I am not what you'd call an "art lover." I feel about art the same way I feel about claymation and zucchini. Picasso's *Dora Maar*? Her face is on backwards. *American Gothic*? Very unattractive farmers. *Whistler's Mother*? She looks like she's been watching *Jeopardy* for 25 years with constipation. The only painting I understand is *Dogs Playing Poker*.

I don't have a problem with other people viewing art. The problem is when they try to force me. Especially to see the Dutch masters, and more especially because most people don't know of my troubled past. Unfortunately, most of my stories begin with my troubled past. And at the center of this troubled past was the DIA.

As a young girl, I had often been taken by my dad to the DIA—a kind of field trip of the macabre. Art wasn't his hobby; he was enrolled in a required class as part of this Business degree from Wayne State University. Had he been studying culinary arts, we would have toured the Wonder Bread factory.

Dad thought it would be nice to take his two daughters along to the museum while he studied— maybe bringing us a little culture. And he would have been right, had it not been for all that blood.

Unluckily for me, my dad's passion was "The Passion"—Christ's suffering, not the fruit. He spent countless hours poring over paintings depicting human torture. Crowns of thorns, crucifixions, floggings—the brutality was captured on canvas with buckets of red paint. Enough red paint, in fact, to cause this young girl to wet herself and weep in fear and sadness. I found no beauty—art or otherwise—in the killing of Jesus.

Again With the Voice

I didn't want to see Rembrandt, honor my little voice, or delve into my long-hidden fears. I was still processing the Sapphic Mass and Gretchen of the Sandals. I had done more spiritual exploration in the last two months than I had in 40 years. People who know me, know that I move at a much slower pace—like a receding ice cap.

As for Rembrandt, if he was so great, why didn't he have a Teenage Mutant Ninja Turtle named after him? Even Donatello had one of those.

Looking for a way out, I talked again with Mark, even sharing the struggle with my little voice. And just like that—just like my partner had done in my battle with Midnight Mass—Mark said, "I shall go with you."

Okay, maybe he didn't say "shall," but he said he'd take me, and he did.

With him, I embarked upon my spiritual hat trick.

Bring Lunch Money

It was Mark's third or fourth trip to see Jesus at the DIA. Face it, his type lives for stuff like that. Mark prefaced our visit by saying the exhibit would be nothing I expected. I, of course, did not believe him. Jesus was Jesus, blood was blood.

We started our afternoon with a quick lunch. Editor's note: Every activity with a 24 year old guy starts with food. Lots. Then my private escort guided me through 64 paintings showing the evolution in Rembrandt's portrayal of Jesus. I was braced for the brutal persecution, the crucifixion and the blood.

That was not what I saw. What I did see was the smashing of another reality. For the first time, I began to see me in Christ. And Christ in me.

You Look Like Jesus, on Your Mother's Side

The exhibit began by explaining how painters before Rembrandt's time were specifically instructed by the Catholic Church how to depict Jesus. Being an obedient young artist, Rembrandt's initial renderings conformed to Rome and that of his contemporaries. But then something changed and everything changed.

Rembrandt moved to Amsterdam during its Golden Age, living and working in the city's vibrant Jewish neighborhood. He assimilated the faces of his neighbors into his character studies and in mid-1640, Rembrandt began to present Jesus as Jewish.

Moreover, Rembrandt parted from the church's directive and began painting Jesus as he saw Him—vulnerable and humble, but also reverent. While Jesus' facial features morphed from gentile to Jew, Rembrandt imagined Jesus as human and divine. Both man and God.

"He discovered God in us," experts write of Rembrandt's work. "He revealed the human essence to a depth known only as divinity."

What caused Rembrandt to change the face of Christ? Some believe he was motivated by historical accuracy. Others believe Rembrandt was evolving with his art—

that his craft was reflective of his own spiritual awakening.

Maybe that old Rembrandt was listening to his little voice, too.

Are You in There?

I've looked high and low for God. I've looked in books and in churches and in people as seemingly lost as me.

Maybe looking for God is like the ocean looking for water.

Maybe God resides in the most sacred place of all.
Inside my little voice.

TLL

Ken

I always wanted a Ken. I didn't want to be Ken and I certainly didn't want to do Ken. I wanted a Ken doll. He was the only doll—and I mean that literally—I ever owned. No little Charlotte holding fake babies crying fake tears and peeing fake, well, pee. We were exclusive—just Ken and me. My Ken, circa 1962, was state-of-the-art injection molded hard plastic, with sexually ambiguous genitalia and fake brunette hair—also molded—into a perfect crew cut, but missing a fleck of paint that came off when I threw him at my sister, missed, and hit a concrete patio block instead.

I found Ken curiously appealing with his pasty white skin, devoid of any muscle definition, non-bendable appendages, and wearing his original candy striped beach jacket and red cotton shorts. That early Ken was a milquetoast man-child, so underdeveloped none of his original apparel—the tennis togs and the wedding tux and the letterman sweater—fit the much later issued sunning, surfing, brawny, blond and bendy Malibu version. Ken, aka Mr. Barbie for 43 years, was lucky enough to take her to the prom and on sexy ski weekends, who starred with her in the Nutcracker ballet, always content to get second billing, never owning a Corvette or dream house of his very own.

Ken, the eternal Richard Burton to Barbie's Elizabeth Taylor, Antony to her Cleopatra, the Guy Richie to her Material Girl. And finally Ken, who was—after nearly a half-century of beguiling Barbie bliss—dumped and emasculated by his better-known better half because, according to her Mattel spokesman, "The flame had gone out of their relationship."

What flame? They were made of vinyl.

I wonder if there is such a thing as dollimony? After more than four decades of attending to her every fancy, Ken was left without the mansion in Malibu, without the Mini Cooper Convertible or VW Microbus, without the musical canopy dream bed or any of the fashion fever furniture, without any of the 42 pets, and still desperately without the promise of a pink plastic penis, and with it the hope of finally consummating love.

Back in the Summer of '69

Growing up in Downriver Detroit, I was the only one I knew with a Ken. Everyone else, and by everyone I mean my sister, the two girls who lived next door, my sister's older friend who watched the original Dark Shadows, and possibly the girl on the corner of our court we befriended exclusively in the summer because she had a pool, was strictly Barbie. Possibly accompanied by Stacie, Skipper, Steffie or ethnically diverse Christie. But Barbie was the headliner.

Me, I couldn't even imagine owning a Barbie. I was too intimidated by her. Her and her demure sideways glance. Her topknot ponytail. Her perfectly pursed and painted lips. And that acrylic stand she straddled. It disappeared somewhere between her secret place and made me weak with wonder. I couldn't bear to dress her or—God-forbid—undress her, couldn't manipulate her appendages or talk her sassy Barbie-speak: "Let's have a campfire!" "Meet me at the mall?"

Never. Ken and I just carried her bags and moved around furniture in that enormous townhouse and kept fuel in her fleet of gas-guzzling pink vehicles.

Yes, I'm out. Barbie was my first true love—with her long legs, tiny waist, ample bosom, slender neck and perfectly flowing blonde locks. Whose appealing yet disproportionate figure became an unattainable icon for all young women growing up in the '60s and '70s. And who inspired generations of women to become Starfleet officers, diplomatic attaches, paratroopers, cowgirls, aerobics instructors, pop singers, pet stylists and anorexics. And, of course, lesbians.

Who cares that if she were a real person, Barbie's measurements would be an impossible 39"-19"-33" or that she'd be 6 feet tall, weigh 100 pounds, and wear a size 4? I would have comforted her through the excruciating back surgeries required to repair the damage done by her top-heavy proportions.

I dated a Barbie look-alike in early recovery (emphasis on early, not recovery.) She was a dead ringer for the vintage '60s doll—all leggy and booby and bouncy and blonde. She even had perfect posture and without the aid of anything foreign forced up her ass. At last, I had my very own Barbie to play with. There's really no reason for me to include this footnote except to brag. And to say that all of my nine-year-old fantasies finally came true. For about 34 seconds. Then she sobered up, came to her senses and dumped me. At that moment, I wished—like Ken—I had had a heart made of synthetic polymers and a rubber head I could pop off and toss away.

This Old Man

While looking for mouse carcasses in the basement last month, I unwittingly unearthed Ken's original tomb. The poor guy was in one of the last remaining boxes I saved marked "mementos." I'm not one to keep clutter. You won't find any of my Girl Scout uniforms or wedding photos lying around. I don't get sentimental over old love letters or baby teeth or the hand-print ashtray I made in second grade. That I still had original Ken surprised me, and delighted me, truth be told.

The old man looked pretty good. He's held up remarkably well, better than me, one might say. To my credit, he hasn't been out of a box in about 35 years. I'd like to see Ken after a trip to rehab, a couple of bad years in the stock market, corporate downsizing, and the invention of something called the "extra value meal."

I put Ken back in his time capsule, in the dreamy world of timeless fictional romance. In that place he would forever be Barbie's. And mine.

TLL

Humbug and Other Tales of Christmas

Since my early 20's, I have come to welcome Christmas much like Ebenezer Scrooge—before the visit from his deceased financial partner and other spirits.

It wasn't always that way. I have the fondest memories of Christmases as a child, starting from the moment my dad ushered in the season with a festive green bulb in our front-porch light. I remember mangers and garland and a plastic Advent wreath. While the requisite prayers were never said, its candles supplied the loveliest light for four weeks of my mother's over-salted meals leading to Dec. 25.

I helped decorate the fireplace mantle and—upon reaching appropriate age—the artificial Christmas tree my parents had purchased their first year of marriage. The yard was strewn with twinkling lights and faux Christmas candles that, like our giant plastic Frosty, never melted. We had reindeer with articulating heads that pranksters, one year, rearranged to demonstrate how baby reindeer were conceived. We would pile into the car after supper to look at the neighborhood lighting displays and return to watch Charlie Brown take pity on the world's most pathetic tree.

Every Christmas Eve my parents hosted my grandmother and her circle of friends for dinner and merriment. These elders had met on their first trans-Atlantic crossing from Germany to America in 1938. We called these people tante and uncle without sharing a common bloodline. They were the people I knew as my family, a hearty group of transplants recreating in southeast Michigan what they had left in Wiesbaden, Mannheim and Stuttgartt.

On December 24 we opened our home to these proud new Americans with thick German accents and odd German traditions. We sang "O Tannenbaum," ate rich foods with funny sounding names like *Weihnachtsplätzchen* and *rollmops*, and served breads so dense they could anchor an ocean liner.

The highlight of the night was what Germans call the *spaziergang*. After our meal, the men, and my sister and I, would bundle up and go for a brisk walk around the block. During this exercise—without fail from year to year—one of the men in our group would spot Santa's sleigh. Uncle Fritz or Uncle Heinrich would pause, point a gloved finger high in the sky, and shout with well-acted excitement, "Look it's Sinterklaas" (Santa Claus). Immediately following, someone else in the group would reach in a pocket and shake a hidden jingle bell. "Und dat's der Rudolph," another would cry. The men would ooh and aah in feigned surprise while my sister and I squealed like little piggies until my dad would finally announce, "We'd better get home to see if Santa's left you girls anything."

Only much later did I learn the entire performance was staged for sheer logistical convenience. Our German aunts and uncles had brought presents they wanted us to open, but under the ruse that they had actually been delivered by Santa. Therefore, someone concocted the idea of the annual spaziergang, during which time my mother and Oma placed the gifts under the tree, while the other women cleaned the kitchen as only German women can. They likely scrubbed the floors and bleached my father's undershorts just for fun.

We'd return to a home smelling of fresh coffee and Clorox, and be surprised to learn that indeed St. Nick had left an impressive pile of presents that my sister and I tore open in delight. There were bags of Weinsnachstgeld—chocolate stamped coins sealed in beautiful gold foil—and other delicacies purchased from the German import store in East Detroit. Every year my sister and I would get a Steiff stuffed toy and a heavy wool coat that Oma had lugged back from her annual trip to Germany because—God knows—you couldn't get a proper winter coat in Michigan. One year I received a black cape with red satin lining that must have weighed 20 pounds. I wore it proudly, even if it made me look like a third grade version of the Phantom of the Opera.

In a cocoon of love we laughed and sang and ate until our bellies nearly burst and our eyelids could stay open no longer. When my sister and I were finally carried off to our beds, our company would start their long car rides back across town: Our Christmas Eve tradition safe for another year.

A Long Winter's Nap

The next morning my family would awake early for mass at St. Cyprians, a practice that would happen less frequently over time. We'd return home for a light breakfast and then came even more gifts. There were Lincoln Logs made of real wood, a bright orange Hot Wheels track with 360° loop, and the cowgirl Jane West. This doll was the fastest female gun in the west and definitely a lesbian pioneer. You could tell by her spurs.

The very best toy of my entire childhood arrived Christmas Day, 1968: The Elly and Andy Mouse Tree House. Elly and Andy were three-inch mouse siblings who lived in a very cozy two-story tree trunk that featured a working elevator. The furnishings included a mushroom dining table and tree-stump chairs that were notched out in back to accommodate the sibling's tails.

Christmases of my childhood delivered on the promise of comfort and joy. They were a time of wonder and possibility, and dreams that came true in every conceivable shape and color. It was a time before the season became synonymous with drinking and fighting and the terror of being left alone. I felt loved and safe, just like Elly and Andy in their perfect little tree-trunk home. I was part of a family that cared for me and that I believed would last forever.

As I grew older, I learned—as we all do—that nothing lasts forever. Not the wonder or the magic or the feeling of being safe. Like a Christmas tree kept too long, my holidays no longer resembled their former selves. My father's drinking escalated, the Germans stopped visiting, and my sister left home. No one was eating *weisswurst* or spotting Santa's sleigh or sleeping in heavenly peace.

The Nightmare Before Christmas

The tipping point, when Christmas officially died for me, was the year my first girlfriend left me. She had tried to break free of our secret, toxic relationship for years. I never believed she would, or could, but apparently six years was her limit. She had someone else to love and love her in return. She was moving on.

It was a tragic cliché. Late on Christmas Eve, Robin arrived on our family's front porch and rang the bell. She was gone by the time my father reached the door. He returned from the front hall carrying a beautifully wrapped box with a gift tag bearing my name. Inside was a butcher block holding six German cooking knives and a note saying goodbye.

Touché.

I went to my room to muffle my sobs. I could share my loss with no one. I was 23 with nothing possibly left to live for. Not the artificial tree, nor the chocolate coins, nor the possibility of hope. On that night some 30 years ago the spirit of Christmas was extinguished.

You must know that my world was very small back then and she was the enormous center. Without Robin I ceased to exist. I had denied everything else to be part of our closeted relationship. Most of all, myself. For days I didn't eat. I didn't sleep. And I certainly didn't celebrate the birth of God's Son as Linus had instructed me in his moving pageant soliloquy.

Recognizing the pall I had cast on the holiday, I finally managed an, "I'm sorry," to my dad weeks later.

Ever the comforting soul, my dad said very softly and very kindly, "It's okay, just so long as you know you ruined Christmas for everyone."

From that year, Christmas mocked me. From the first bell ringer to the onslaught of radio ads touting "the gift she'll love forever" to the bombardment of glad tidings, Christmas assailed me while masquerading as cheer.

I'm Just Getting Started ...

On Dec. 25, 1992, my Oma—my very best friend since birth—died. Within the course of 30 days, she had gone from living independently in her second-floor condo, a standing weekly appointment at the nearby hair salon and driving a brand new Chevrolet sports coupe, to dying alone in Wyandotte General Hospital.

From the moment her health began to fail, I was with Oma as often as I could. While I begged my parents to allow Oma to finish her days at my home in Rochester, they insisted on placing her in a nursing facility Downriver. I would visit, recounting tales of those special Christmas Eve celebrations we shared. She was finally moved to the hospital Dec. 23, and I was determined to be with her at the end. But at 4:00 p.m. on Christmas day, my dad instructed me to come home to salvage what few hours remained of Christmas.

Ever the perfect daughter, I did as instructed. The phone rang almost immediately as I walked through the door. It was the hospital saying Oma had just passed. I wasn't there to hold her hand and say goodbye.

While others were making merry I was making arrangements at Martensen's funeral home.

In the years since my grandmother's death, I've had a ridiculous collection of losses in December. They include—and not necessarily in this order—the death of my first AA sponsor, getting dumped by my second girlfriend, the death of my dog Murphy, and one monumental relapse (January 1).

Then in 2006, my father died December 21.

Death, Take a Number

I'm embarrassed to say I wasn't overly distraught at my dad's death. First, because the two of us weren't on the greatest of terms. Second, tragedy had become a familiar part of my annual holiday season.

My dad's passing happened even more quickly than Oma's. He had apparently driven himself to Wyandotte General in mid-December because he reported, "not feeling quite right." Doctors admitted him immediately. His undiagnosed condition worsened each day until he was placed on life support—the very machines his will specified not be used to extend his life.

I was in Louisville on a job interview. My brother-in-law, a man who had never before and has not since, called to say I needed to get on the first plane back to Detroit. I returned in time to argue with my sister, mother, and his doctors, produce my dad's living will, and help him to die peacefully and naturally as he and God intended. I sat with him alone as he took his last breath, ten days after he entered the hospital.

Christmas Day found our very small family at the same funeral home where more than a dozen years earlier my Oma was laid to rest.

The Christmas Massacre Continues

Now, despite the presence of my partner and her family to assuage my holiday blues, I continue my assault on Christmas. I decorate the holiday with equal parts holly and contempt. Unlike the 20-something Charlotte who suffered her loss in silence, I toast the season with a frothy cup of egregious distain. I often wish to join the long list of those I've loved and lost, as I'm sure those near me wish as well. My father's words return with newfound truth, "You know you've ruined Christmas for everyone."

I feel no remorse. It is my song of the season.

But Wait, There's More

Five months ago I pulled into my driveway after an unremarkable day at the office, a usual Michigan Monday in late December—cold, dark and still. A few neighbors had begun to festoon their homes in celebration of Christmas—a hodgepodge of secular and non-secular displays, each set upon a canvas of hideous halogen lights. Even our own home—thanks exclusively to my partner—began to resemble a 1920s Rockwell drawing. A fresh wreath sprayed across the front door, a seven-foot tree tickled the ceiling of our tea room, and cedar garland twirled around the banister.

The headlights of my SUV hit the scene like a movie set. I half expected to see Darren McGavin in the window fondling a very fragile leg-shaped lamp wrapped in a fishnet stocking. But instead I was shocked by something quite different: a FOR SALE sign planted dramatically in the center of my neighbor's front lawn. A new Christmas tragedy was being delivered to me and right on time.

I parked, and instead of going into my house, I walked directly to Agnes' front door and banged loudly. She answered wearing a tear-stained flannel robe.

"What the fuck?" I shouted in disbelief.

She gestured me inside. Her enormous cat Sammy was stretched out on the radiator, nonplussed by my coarse greeting. The question hung in the air, not to be answered. My next-door neighbor, the woman who had vexed me and comforted me and was my surrogate

221

mother for nearly ten years, was finished. Her age, health, and deteriorating 90-year-old house pointed to one thing: It was time to move on.

For her, the time had been coming for several years. In the recesses of my consciousness I guess I knew as well. But nothing says finality like a for sale sign. It was a tombstone punctuating "the end." She would be living with her daughter in South Carolina, not at all a place I imagined visiting with any frequency. Or ever wanting to.

Her house sold in a week, and she was determined to leave our sleepy hamlet a very short time thereafter. There were estate sales and movers and a flurry of children with their fingers in the pie—some I had never seen in all of my time as the neighbor.

Agnes, who began our relationship by painting a red line down the center of our shared driveway and cursing me not to cross it, had become a member of my family. Like the German aunts and uncles with whom I shared no DNA, this cranky, caring, annoying, accepting woman became a relative. And as God's perfect plan had prescribed, she would fill the void left by my own estranged mother. Agnes was yet another part of my zany sitcom family—the nutty neighbor who spent her days peering through half-drawn blinds and poking her nose in my not-so-private business.

Every part of her made every part of me crazy. I'm sure the opposite was true in spades. She was an 80-something agnostic with bad knees; me—a God-fearing drunk who sleeps with women. But somehow the 20 feet of asphalt separating her side door from mine became a great equalizer. It bridged generational norms, traditional values and everything else that was logically meant to keep us apart—even our Michigan/Michigan State rivalry. Our dance—of loving and fighting, laughing and yelling, comforting and attending to and being present for—worked. Her children knew it, my partner knew it, and all were thankful for it.

I surrendered rather than fought the move. I kept my distance and let the dervishes whirl. In our final visit the three of us—Agnes, my partner Sharon, and I—spent a quiet hour together on Christmas Day exchanging small gifts. Sharon did her best to carry the conversation, Agnes wept, and I was paralyzed with sadness.

A short time after, she was gone.

My friends, the people who claim to understand me, were comforting or annoying or both. They said all the expected things like, "You were lucky to have had her in your life," and, "You can visit her whenever you want." Those less enlightened said, "Well, I bet you're glad to have her out of your hair." More than one said, "Prepare for Agnes to die. Elderly people often pass away quickly after being uprooted from their homes."

But she was already dead to me—real or imagined. She had been the stalwart of the neighborhood, the woman who bought my coffee cream and fed my cats and loaned me every tool out of her garage. And opened her heart so that I might find a very safe corner of unconditional love.

Aren't You Just a Saint?

Those who knew Agnes and were familiar with our relationship recognized me (and Sharon) for allowing her to perhaps live in her home longer that she could have without us. After all, weren't we the ones with the impressive list of altruistic acts like shoveling her snow and flipping her mattresses and visiting every day to check her pulse?

I won't lie, I often boasted about the extraordinary care I provided for my feeble, elderly neighbor as if I were some modern day Clara Barton. In my retelling of the "woman next-door story," I was clearly the superhero, a lesbian Wonder Woman for helpless octogenarians. But my stories are rarely accurate, and I'm never quite as herculean as I claim. In fact, if there were a true hero in this story, it was her.

Agnes was much more my caretaker than I hers. Sure, it's easy to point to grand gestures—how I lifted things and opened things and read the stuff written in really small type. But grand gestures are merely window dressing. Agnes accepted me—the impatient misfit with an ill-mannered dog who uprooted her annuals—despite 80 years of being instructed otherwise. She held my hand and made me Swedish meatballs and weeded the cracks in the driveway. Even on my side of the red line.

It's not hyperbole to say I miss her every single day. Every exhausting, delightful, irritating, generous, hilarious thing about her. But what I miss most is always knowing she is right next door. My ever loving lighthouse keeper.

A Dickens of a Time

So once again I swear at God, "Why do you take them from me, all of the people I love most? And why must I suffer these tragedies at Christmas?"

Like Mr. Scrooge, I most fear the ghost of Christmas future. Not of things that have come but of those yet to be. I can only expect the familiar toll of anguish to ring through future holidays and batter my senses with grief and death. It is the chain I forge in life, link by link, loss by loss.

But as ghost Marley tells Scrooge, if I heed the visits of the specters and amend my earthly ways, I can change the future. I can escape the inevitable suffering meant for me. Therefore, I take this challenge to my therapist, the same woman who for years has cobbled me together after holidays filled with despair. I tell her about Agnes, the pain, the familiar pattern of abandonment, the loneliness, the hopelessness, and the unsolved mystery of why.

She is familiar with the script and has heard it far too many times. The endless wailing, the self-pity and the resentment. It is my Christmas carol, "Woe is me, life's unfair, Tiny Tim will die, fa la la la la, la la, la, la."

225

But in this visit the refrain is different.

"I want to stop," I say to her, surprised at my own words.

I want to stop the pattern. Change the narrative. End the melancholy, the dread, the feeling sorry for myself, the sitting in pity—the sucking the joy from the holiday and ruining it for everyone around me. I want to stop hating Christmas. And I want it to stop hating me back. Considering Christmas is an annual occurrence, and I expect to be around for another 20 or so years, it seems the sensible thing to do. It's truly amazing how often "sensible" evades me.

"I don't want to be taken hostage by my emotions for six weeks of every year," I say to my therapist Diane. "I'm tired of feeling the way I feel."

"And how's that?" she asks.

"Empty and abandoned," I say. "Like everyone else on earth is having a great time celebrating the joys of the season and I'm stuck in a Christmas time-out."

"Well, not everyone," she says.

"How so?"

"Well, imagine yourself nine months' pregnant, riding around on a donkey and looking for a place to spend the night. You're exhausted, but you keep getting turned away by judgmental innkeepers. On top of that, the child you bear is of an immaculate conception. I can't expect that was a picnic."

My therapist uses a rich blend of spirituality, psychology, intellect, common sense, recovery, Jesus,

226

and goading to reach me. While I appreciate her technique, I understand it might not be for everyone.

"Seriously, I've got a 30-year history of holiday death and dying and you're pulling out the Virgin Mary?" I question. "Is that really the best you've got?"

"Well, you said that Christmas is a time of great joy and celebration for everyone."

This, I believe, is clearly in the goading category.

"So the Virgin Mary had it worse off than me?" I ask sarcastically. "That is my big take away?"

"It really isn't a matter of better or worse. It's a matter of consciousness. Since Robin left you, you've held a belief that a person's presence—or lack thereof—in your life is somehow a reflection of your worth. When people move on, you feel abandoned and rejected, and you turn that against yourself.

"You run these alternative scenarios that suggest if you'd done something different—been something different—that people wouldn't leave you. But the truth is people don't leave because of you. People move on because of them.

"Just like Mary, you feel uncomfortable and confused. You feel rejected. But the miracle is about to happen."

She beamed with satisfaction. I truly hate the beaming.

"I'm going to have a baby in a cow barn and name him Jesus?"

"You can birth a new consciousness," she said. "You can choose to view your life as a series of miracles.

Every person who has entered your life is a gift. Robin, your grandmother, Agnes, your father, your sponsor—each has given you gifts to treasure for a lifetime. When they move on, it is a time to celebrate and even share those gifts—those Christmas presents. God gave the world His most precious gift on Christmas day. You've gotten your most precious gifts during the holiday season. You have the ability to release your old thinking about what you believe to be loss and rejoice in the gifts you've been given."

That was a lot to process. A virgin, a donkey, and a lesbian. Like the beginning of a bad joke.

"Don't get me wrong," she said. "You'll still experience sadness. But you can invite in a new perspective to help you prepare for the miracles yet to come your way. Every time God closes a door He opens a window."

The thought of a new nosy neighbor wiggling through my kitchen window made me wince.

"So, a life of pain and suffering can be over just like that?" I snapped my fingers.

"It's about willingness." She smiled. "Just like when you stopped drinking. If you are indeed willing to change, willing to release the pain and accept God's will for your life, you can begin Christmas anew.

"Thank God for taking such good care of Agnes by giving her a safe and loving home. Thank Him for the lessons she has brought forth and her presence in your life. Then pray for a miracle. A new spirit to enter your life. A new way to be of service and share your gifts."

"But people aren't Legos," I argue. "We aren't commodities. When someone drops dead or stops loving you or moves away we don't just call central casting and ask for a replacement."

"And isn't that a blessing?" she was quick to respond. "God puts new people in our lives to continue our learning. With Robin you learned how to fully express your love. From Oma you learned the unconditional love of family. And because learning is a long-long journey, God provided Agnes, who lets you experience both receiving and giving love, far from anything you've ever known before.

"God cares so much for you, he puts people in your life to teach you your importance. It's your job now to carry God's love to others, as a reflection of His love for them."

Willingness in Action, Take One

My peonies are in full bloom, heralding the arrival of summer. More than five months have passed since Agnes' move. My partner and I Skype with her every Sunday at noon; Agnes and I speak on the phone nearly every day. Our bond is stronger than ever.

I've said hello a few times to the new folks living next door. There appears no instant chemistry. So far there's been no new red paint. That's a good thing. I'll remain open to whatever happens. I remember it's all about perspective.

I feel Agnes with me as I work in the garden; I have her old lawnmower and shovels. They are a great comfort to me. My fat dog, the one she loved so much, rolls in the grass nearby. I send her photos of everything. I might buy a plane ticket for the fall.

Diane is right, I miss Agnes like crazy. Sharon holds my hand when I cry, which is often. I force myself to remember what I know to be true: Agnes is very much alive, driving her poor daughter crazy some 868 miles away. She's safe and cared for, and very much loved.

I'm safe and cared for too, and loved a lot more than I knew possible ten years ago. I dry my tears and can't believe my luck. To misquote a favorite old movie, "Of all the gin joints in all the towns in all the worlds," I was blessed to walk into hers. For a decade I went to school every day in her classroom, learning about life and love over BLTs and icy cold root beers.

Is This Considered Re-Gifting?

If I took all the gifts I'd been given over my many years and combined them all together, imagine what a miracle that would be. A Christmas present for the ages; an enormous box filled with gratitude and kindness, comfort and joy. All wrapped in love. And smelling like a fresh cut pine and warm apple strudel.

I'd like to make that my gift to mankind all year long. It's a way to honor my many teachers and the lessons they brought me, hard at times though some were. In that way their beauty and their wisdom live on for lifetimes to come.

If I do as Diane suggests, have willingness and invite miracles, I'm guessing more gifts are in store for me. I'm open to that. To tearing back the curtains, shouting out the widow and rejoicing in the season. It'd be nice for a change, to be light as a feather, happy as an angel, merry as a schoolgirl.

Perhaps I will start today. June 7 is as good a day as any to begin celebrating Christmas. Considering what a pill I've been for the last 30 years, the sooner I get started the better.

So if you hear me wishing you a Merry Christmas and the calendar says otherwise, please just go with it. Tip your hat and smile at the slightly delirious woman who has just birthed a new consciousness. Today I'm inviting the love of all the spirits to flow through me for God's greatest good. It's a celebration that would make old Fezziwig proud.

TLL

Typeface

I was reading a book the other day in which the author and her friend were comparing their "types." Hers was Jake Gyllenhaal—the classic dark, brooding and tortured male; the BFF's was a sinewy, tattooed and underfed Adam Levine. A friend of mine says her type is anyone breathing. I don't think she's even that picky.

I've known I'm the "girls" type pretty much my entire life. Apparently, every man and every woman have 22 pairs of chromosomes plus one pair that defines sex. Females have two X chromosomes; males have an X and a Y. Perhaps my second X fell off the page. Perhaps I'm actually the typo type.

It's hard for me to understand the purpose of declaring a type, like a college major. My "type" has always been the classic Barbie, which sounds lame and possibly cliché coming from a 52-year old woman with three cats. Okay, seven cats.

My partner Sharon is not the ubiquitous blonde bombshell and is, therefore, theoretically not my type. She is, however, completely out of my league. People take one look at Sharon, then me, and figure I must be extremely wealthy with an imminent life-ending illness. Or, that she lost a bet.

232

It is very awkward going through life when your partner is the much more appealing part of the set. She's definitely the salt. There isn't a day that goes by she isn't hit on—most of the time while I'm standing right next to her. A man or woman will shamelessly flirt with her, suggestively commenting on her eyes or her smile or the unique color of her hair. I'll put my hand possessively on Sharon's shoulder and announce, "She's with me." Then I'll be dismissed like an inexpensive cut of beef. If ever we are both involved in a severe car accident, I doubt the paramedics will notice me enough to cut me out of my seat belt and take me to the hospital. Even with a severed head, Sharon is likely to be much more attractive.

My girlfriend has been mistaken for a young Julianne Moore on more than one occasion. And actress Jodie Foster—but before she started co-starring in movies with children. I've only been mistaken as the woman who mops up dog urine at PetSmart. Since Sharon doesn't resemble the archetypal Barbie, I am led to believe all this hooey about type is just that. One friend, for example, describes her type as Viggo Mortensen. Her husband of 25 years looks like the French cousin of the Elias Brothers' "Big Boy." As the kids say, "WTF?"

I once went out with a woman who had been institutionalized on 13 separate occasions for mental illness. When she told me she wasn't interested in going out with me a second time, I was actually distraught. You'd think *that* would have made me exactly her type.

Oops, Is That Your Boob?

In my 30s I ran away from home to work for an American company in Japan. I was immediately assigned a local 20-something female assistant with a slightly wide bottom and unfortunate taste in shoes. This Gal Friday was not my type. She did, however, excel in helping me with local customs, language, cuisine and her country's web of high-speed trains. She could also sniff out alcohol like a Samurai blood hound. There wasn't an evening of drinking that didn't end in the wee hours of the next day—often revisiting the previous night's sushi for a second or third time.

During my assignment in Tokyo I stayed in a spacious "western-style" hotel: Western meaning not one of those miniature capsules the size of a cat carrier and rented by the minute through vending machines.

The hotel offered many luxuries: housekeeping, room service, a personal laundress and access to a 24-hour bartender. The hotel bar was our usual last stop after a marathon night of clubbing. One morning, in the pre-dawn haze of inebriation, my international assistant announced that she wanted to see my bed. This was a new development. She had, until then, shown no apparent interest in me, unless her subtle overtures had been lost in translation.

She sat perched on my lap, drinking sake from my cup and running her fingers through my thick blonde American hair. We were in a shameless tangle, nuzzling each other like two exotic birds. That she was not my

234

type became irrelevant. I would not deny this woman merely because she looked like Barbie's Asian friend *Kira*.

"I want to see your bed," she insisted in a heavily slurred accent. While someone else might have misinterpreted, bed is a word I don't get wrong. In any language.

We extracted ourselves from the plush lounger and stumbled to the bank of elevators, spilling the last of our drinks as we went. She searched my pockets for the room's key card as we rode up 16 floors. We somehow found my room in the high-rise labyrinth. Then, in one deliberate move, I slid the door open, reached for a small breast and lunged at her mouth like an anteater embarking upon its final meal.

"No! No! No! What are you doing?" she screamed, as she fell back and shook herself free of my invasion.

"What?" I cried. "What? What? You said you wanted to see my bed. You. My. Bed."

"Yes, bed," she explained, suddenly remarkably sober. "I want to see your bed. Bed. I heard they have big size western king bed in rooms here. I never have seen before."

I was told later by a knowledgeable and seasoned lesbian that some women, even extremely straight married women, can become very touchy, very flirty and very playful when they're drunk. These actions, she insisted, should never be mistaken as an invitation for sex. Never.

Fortunately, that was the first and only time I ever made a sexual "advance" toward a woman—a one-off mistake of epic proportion. As a footnote to the story, I'll never, ever be returning to Japan. At least that's what I told the U.S. Embassy there.

Beautiful Men, Still Not My Type

I hate to sound prejudiced, but men are never my type. There are men I love—dear friends who are like the brothers I never had. And men I find attractive—usually a subset of chubby guys with unruly hair, who make me laugh and know their way around a charcoal grill. But that is as far as it goes. I am not cosmopolitan enough to play "both sides" of the sexual meridian.

Once, while still masquerading as a heterosexual, I got roped into going on a blind date with a male co-worker's male cousin. Repeatedly I staved off the invitation, but after weeks of his nagging, I finally gave in. It was, you can image, a fiasco of *Will & Grace* proportion.

When I arrived at the restaurant to meet the cousin, along with my co-worker and his wife—who were a non-negotiable requirement of the deal—the co-worker and his wife were no shows. At that moment I should have turned on my heels and left. But the cousin was already flagging me with his napkin as if I had won the Indy 500.

How bad can one meal be? I thought.

The answer: "Really, really bad."

I don't remember Giuseppe being an unattractive man. That he was a man, however, doomed our little outing from the start.

Giuseppe was swarthy, like a pirate or a person who'd been held in a prison camp for months. He enjoyed gesturing with his hands, as if "signing" our date for the hearing impaired. Like many men are given to do, Giuseppe had bathed himself in cologne, enough to overpower the smell of grease and garlic emanating from the kitchen. For that I was almost thankful.

I took command of the conversation, peppering him with banal and annoying questions. Where do you live? Where did you go to school? Where do you work? Where did you buy those shoes?

My answers for those same questions were forthright and prideful: Expensive suburb, working on my MBA, Fortune 500, blah blah blah, me me me. The date took place during a time in my life I when I was extremely egocentric, as opposed to later when I became totally consumed with my narcissism.

His answers were cagier. He'd moved around a lot, attended several schools and worked a number of odd jobs. Nothing was formed in concrete, except—I suspected—much of his family's home.

"What are your goals?" I queried. "Where do you see yourself, long term?

I was more of an obnoxious guidance counselor than polite dinner companion.

"Hmmm," he groaned, "Not sure, possibly the restaurant business."

"Well, that certainly is ambitious." I perked up. "Having your own restaurant is very demanding."

"Probably not owning my own place," he interrupted, "At least not right away. In fact, I've got a pretty good gig going right now."

"Gig?" I questioned. No one in my yuppie circle of tight assed friends had gigs. Gigs were not had, unless you were a 1920s jazz musician.

"Yeah," he continued, "I'm working at a pizza joint. Maybe you've heard of it—'Chuckie Cheese?'"

At that point every blood vessel in my body seized up like Labor Day traffic through the Detroit-Windsor tunnel.

Chuckie Cheese, also known as Chuck E. Cheese's Pizza Time Theatre, is a restaurant/arcade nightmare. The highlight is an animatronic animal band fronted by Chuck—an anthropomorphic mouse.

For those of you who've never been there, Chuckie Cheese is where singing hippos and dancing bears go to die. Taking children to Chuckie Cheese is like taking a bag of squirrels to a dog park and letting the squirrels go free. Except at Chuckie Cheese the squirrels are unleashed inside your head.

"You work at Chuckie Cheese?" I sneered with as much derision I could muster.

Please God, I thought. Please have Giuseppe tell me he's the regional marketing manager or chief financial officer or even the guy who cleans the Whac-A-Mole game.

"Yeah," he bragged. "But it's real easy. I just put my head on twice an hour, sing Happy Birthday and hand out a few balloons."

No one should ever utter the words, "I just put my head on."

I was officially on a date with a man who went to work dressed in a rodent suit and likely got his jollies feeling up the nannies and older sisters of unsuspecting 3-year-old birthday celebrants.

I was called a "Bitch" by my coworker when I didn't return Giuseppe's calls.

Now I have a policy: I don't go out with vermin. No possum, no badger, no muskrat. I do date beaver. But that's another story.

U R Not My Type

Who knows what people see in other people? Type, like beauty, must lie in the eye of the beholder. Obviously my girlfriend goes for women with no foreseeable income but who can run a mile in 27.5 minutes. If you want someone to finish off the Sunday leftovers, I'm your girl. I can perform the complete Broadway production of *Les Miserables* using finger puppets. Perhaps I'm an acquired taste.

For many years I looked for a specific type – the "gorgeous, wealthy, can't do enough to fulfill me sexually and enjoys washing dishes afterward" type.

Perhaps that species has become extinct. Like Nessie the Loch Ness monster, I've never found her.

I am currently hooked on the Sandra Bullock type—not so much her type as the actual her. Sharon has no concerns with my pathetic crush because: 1) Sharon has above-average self-esteem and 2) Sharon has seen me flirt. Sandra Bullock is the best combination ever—funny with girl-next-store beauty. If I had a modern-day Frankenstein machine, I'd put Joan Cusack's personality inside Halle Berry's body. Hell, if I had that kind of technology, I'd put me inside her body.

I'd rather have a funny woman than a beautiful one, unless Sofia Vergara is available. Then I would take her, twice.

Does She Come with Instructions?

There is a major misconception within the lesbian community that having sex with another woman comes naturally. Perhaps because we're the same "type," people assume "Woman A" simply pleasures "Woman B" in the same way she herself would want to be pleased. Warning: This is the second worst piece of advice I've ever received. The first was the suggestion that I try sleeping with men.

One can never assume that two people like the same thing—ever. Not restaurants, not movies, not dog breeds, and certainly not what they like in bed. You may find yourself apologetically saying, "Oh, I'm sorry, I thought everyone enjoyed being gagged with a pair of silk stockings while having a vaginal irrigation."

Even worse is having sex with someone of the opposite sex when you're gay. It's like trying to put IKEA furniture together without any instructions. You end up with some extra pieces at the end and the whole thing never quite feels complete.

I was 17 years and 13 days old when I had my first sexual experience. It was the first time for both of us. A lot gets forgiven during your first time. I could have used a Dust Buster and a Johnsonville bratwurst and she still would have thought I was fantastic. It was amusement park sex—a teeny bit scary, with a lot of screaming and flailing. Nothing was clumsy or self aware. Not for a moment did we worry how we compared. We had just invented sex.

Not all sex is like that. Sex with Barbie was like being stranded on a desert island. In our minds, we were the only two survivors of a horrific plane crash. It was exotic and desperate. Unfortunately, I wanted sex like I wanted drugs. In that brief relationship I learned that there was a difference between love and addiction. I didn't, however, learn precisely what it was.

Sexual Dust Bowl

There have been several periods in my life when I've gone for years without sex. For the record, I've had only four sexual partners. That number often shocks people into asking questions such as: "Were you in a prolonged coma?" "Were you a cloistered nun?" "Were you possibly born without a vagina?"

A woman in my book club—a highly spiritual non-alcoholic—tells me her number is seven. I consider her neither a prude nor a slut. Seven is like a lifetime batting average of .317—very respectable. It could very well get her into Cooperstown.

I'm past worrying about my number of sexual partners, or lack thereof. Even if I lie by adding fictitious conquests to my meager list, no one seems to believe most things I say. If at age 52 I claimed to be both a virgin and an investment banker, people would think I'm a whore who works at a car wash.

Use Your Own Equipment

People say the key to sex is being open and honest. I believe honesty should never enter the picture. The real key to sex is always answering "yes." Did you orgasm, yes. Was it the best you ever had, yes. Do you want to cuddle, yes. Do you want cake, yes. Do you want me to invite over my neighbor, the Swedish pole-dancing flight attendant, and her twin sister? God yes.

Despite what women might want you to believe, women—straight and gay—are (for the most part) as crude and horny and irreverent about sex as any man. In fact, the older women get, the smuttier they become. Any woman over 60 will fuck anything younger than 30—a very unfortunate inverse mathematical equation. Don't fool yourself, not all women love with their heads

242

and their hearts, as the saying goes. Much of their thinking comes from below the belt as well.

Master of My Domain

I just read a survey conducted by *Esquire* magazine. Editors tallied up a variety of sexual statistics collected from their female readers, including number of partners, age at time of first encounter, multiples (partners and orgasms), positions and preferences. This particular survey of women showed:

- 69 percent either own or are in the market for a vibrator or other sex toy;
- 60 percent masturbate multiple times a week;
- 40 percent prefer intercourse to cuddling;
- 61 percent occasionally enjoy hard core porn.

This was the first time I'd ever sided with a majority of the respondents in a sex survey. It's nice to finally be part of the mainstream.

Masturbation has gotten a really bad rap throughout the years, which is a real shame. Masturbation is much like speeding. Everybody does it. It is impossible not to. You only feel guilty when you get caught. Even so, you're likely to speed again, maybe later that same afternoon. I have a lot of points on my driving record.

I love the pleasures of the flesh. Mostly my own. I started pleasuring myself regularly at a very young age. Some people play solitaire. I just do it without the cards. Having a healthy masturbation life came in quite handy during my dozen years of marriage.

Masturbation is an irrefutable part of life and a part of our nation's fabric. A page from the 1918 Sears catalog listed a "portable vibrator with attachments" as very "useful and satisfactory for home service." Unfortunately, Sears no longer stocks vibrators in its enormous inventory. Considering the financial position of the once beloved retail giant, perhaps management should consider adding vibrators to the ailing store's line of Craftsman tools. Especially the strap-ons.

Every married mom in my straight 40-and-older crowd is singing (or screaming) the praises of battery-operated self-stimulation. Rather than explore the hidden symbolism in Faulkner's tortured classic *As I Lay Dying* during a recent meeting of my book club, my supposed high-brow literary posse spent the three hours sipping white wine, eating trays of Costco appetizers and comparing vibrator stories.

"Have you tried the one shaped like a rabbit?" asked Minnie. "Its ears curve up and really hit my G-spot."

"My bunny has multiple speeds and glows in the dark," chimed in Karen.

"I had to replace my platinum power bullet three times last summer when Hank went to Mississippi to start up that new Toyota plant," confessed Betty.

"I won't even let my husband touch me with his 'thingy' anymore," said Steph.

"I have a big black latex dildo named Tyrone," boasted a usually shy Lorraine.

"Right in the middle of taking photos of Lindsay and Chad before the Snowball dance last winter my camera died and I had to run upstairs to get the batteries out of my vibrator," laughed Stacey. "Lindsay came into my bedroom to see what was taking so long and completely busted me with it. Now I'm sure everyone at St. Thomas Aquinas is going to know that Mrs. Bellman owns a vibrator. I can't wait to go to the next parent-teacher's conference."

"I heard a story about a dog who found his owner's dildo and started playing with it in the dining room just as she was about to serve supper to her in-laws," said Lori. "I can't believe it, though."

"Believe it," said Minnie. "Buster got a hold of mine once and I had to trade him a rawhide to get it back. Have you ever used a dildo with teeth marks in it?"

Who are these women and when did sex toys replace chicken recipes as appropriate conversation? One can even host home parties where such items are proudly displayed and passed around like smutty hot potatoes. More white wine, more snacks, pull out your credit card and viola, the hostess just won herself a lovely set of vibrating Ben-Wa balls. Tupperware be damned.

Betcha Can't Have Just One

Some years ago, my Barbie look-alike and I were vacationing in the Caymans. I was totally insecure in my ability to satisfy her, being the beautiful woman she was. I'm a firm believer that beautiful women never have mediocre sex. Why would they? It's the same reason beautiful women never pay for drinks or change light bulbs.

So I went to the local Lover's Lane retail store and gathered more armament than a sleeper cell of al-Qaeda terrorists. I washed my various instruments, fitted them with long-life batteries and packed them in my suitcase. When we landed, the tiny island airport was alive with fruit drinks and Tiki music. Our luggage was sitting in a cordoned-off area with other bags that had already been cleared. As I approached the bags, I heard a distinct buzzing sound. I looked for bees. I looked for flies. I looked for someone with a vacuum cleaner or a hand-blender. I noticed that my black Tummi was gyrating ever so slightly. I opened the bag to find every one of our sex toys "on" and having a wild party without us. We'd been punk'd by some wise-cracking customs agent. Barbie and I snickered, shut down the equipment, and hailed a bellman to take our luggage to the cab stand. The only thing Barbie told the driver was, "Can you please stop at a store that sells batteries?"

Of course I couldn't wait to tell this story to my friend—the one who still does sex the prehistoric way with an actual penis. Her pathetic response: "How many of those things do you need?"

At that moment I realized another kind of "type:" The type of people who'd ask a question like that. And me.

TLL

Choice

There was a sophisticated vending machine at my last place of employment that sold an endless variety of snacks—both sugary and salty. Customers were required to press both the number and letter assigned to the corresponding food item to get the desired selection. The process made me a nervous wreck. First I had to choose from a sea of choices—healthy or artery clogging. Then, was I obliged to enter the correct alphanumeric code. It was like disarming a bomb. More often than not I screwed up, punching E12 instead of F1. In horror, I was forced to watch as a metal coil pushed a family-sized bag of jet-puffed pork rinds off the ledge instead of my fat-free Fig Newtons.

A cookie is just a cookie, mind you, but a Newton is fruit and cake.

I would complain to anyone who would listen about the error, but there was no consolation for making a bad choice.

I'll admit, I've made my share of bad choices. But many of my so called "choices"—the ones I'm often known for—weren't choices at all.

I never made the choice to be neurotic or alcoholic or born with a hole in my heart.

And I never chose to be gay.

Many people disagree with me on that last one and that's where my conversation with them begins and ends.

If people believe, as does a large percentage of the global population, that being gay is a choice, there's no opportunity for further discussion. If people believe, like Uganda's David Bahati, that "same sex attraction is not an innate and immutable characteristic," then I'll just go for a long walk and save my breath. Because no really good argument is going to convince these folks that being gay is just another of nature's ways. The dialogue is moot, because the whole time I'm talking about biology and God's will, they're thinking I should pray harder to remove my sexual aberration, or become celibate, or get hypnotized, or take a laxative, or wear looser underwear. Their minds are closed. To them, I'm just a stubborn freak who's gay simply because I want to be. And, by God, I'm going pay for it.

A friend of mine recently told me that choice is the lynchpin of the gay-rights movement. Since obviously blacks didn't choose to be black, and women didn't choose to have ovaries, their road to equality was somewhat less frustrated. In fact, she likens "choice" to "inception" in the debate over abortion. If a person believes that life begins the moment the sperm and egg unite—you are never going to convince them abortion is not murder.

Unfortunately, science cannot provide us with absolutes on many things. Why are some people alcoholics? What makes a person gay? At what precise moment is life created? Where do all the assholes come from? Many of these answers are clouded in morality. People use religion, coercion, medical misinterpretation and psychological hogwash to form irrational conclusions and then try to shove them down the throats of others. Their arguments are flawed: AIDS is God's punishment for homosexuality, gay marriage will lead to bestiality, gays are sexual predators, you can get gay from a public toilet seat.

Here's a news flash: Outlawing homosexual behavior will not make me straight any more than taking away my vodka made me a social drinker. I've been evicted, slapped, ostracized, marginalized and denied a Big Mac because I was gay. Now ask yourself, "What kind of idiot would be gay if they had the choice?"

In the immortal words of Popeye, ""I yam what I yam!"

The same friend told me gay rights is the civil rights movement of our era—our Equal Rights Amendment and Affirmative Action. She reminded me of a time when interracial marriages were illegal. When women couldn't get credit cards in their own names. When a person's physical and mental limitations diminished their right to fully participate in all aspects of society. Equality just got another partner. And can he accessorize!

Laws Don't Change People

Face it, gays are not going to overthrow the government. We're better off designing belts than working inside the beltway. It's going to take a far more concerted effort from LGBT-rights' organizations before politicians begin taking us seriously. Lawmakers pander to constituencies with powerful voting blocs and lots of money. Most elected officials fail to see how adopting a gay-rights agenda is a good thing. Gaining 10 new gay votes is great, but not at the expense of losing 100 homophobic voters.

Gays today are mostly without a voice. No one has replaced Harvey Milk—I'm not sure anyone has even tried. We need fearless and dynamic change agents who will appoint judges, write laws and make good on their campaign promises. That includes enlisting the straight majority to carry our water. More than 10 percent of voters need to go to the polls with a rainbow axe to grind. Then maybe Congress will notice. It won't work by putting minority issues to a majority vote. Successful change happens organically, individually and never overnight.

Education is Key

A positive social movement based on public awareness is necessary for change.

People need to know that in Michigan today it is perfectly legal to fire, refuse to hire, or refuse to promote someone because an employer thinks they are

250

lesbian, gay, bisexual or transgender. It's also legal to deny LGBTers rental housing and refuse them service in stores. The issue of joint adoption is still being negotiated.

People need to know that Michigan's governor objected to extending healthcare benefits to domestic partners of state employees. And that there is no protection against harassment based upon a person's sexual orientation—no specific action for people affected by sexual-orientation based violence.

Further, the Michigan legislature has never amended the Elliot Larson Civil Rights Act of 1976 to include discriminating based on sexual orientation, gender identity or expression. That means gays and lesbians are not protected from education and public service discrimination.

People need to know that same-sex couples, whether married or not, are denied a host of Federal benefits provided to heterosexual married couples, including Social Security survivor benefits, estate and gift tax exemptions, federal tax benefits, veterans benefits, immigration and citizenship status, and other health and retirement benefits for Federal employees.

People need to know that in 2016 in the United States of America, gays are not fully recognized as equal citizens.

That was never my choice.

(Author's note: Not long after this piece was written, two amazing decisions were made. First, the U.S. Supreme Court ruled 5-4 to allow same-sex marriage nationwide. Second, my city of Pleasant Ridge passed a human rights ordinance prohibiting discrimination based on race, color, religion, sex, age, height, weight, marital status, family status, HIV status, national origin, physical or mental disability, sexual orientation or gender identity. To the brave men and women involved in these decisions I say, "Thanks" and, "Good choice!")

TLL

The Necklace

Recently, my partner of several years decided we needed to start dating. The good news is that we'll be dating each other. The bad news is we have to schedule organized activities—engagements, if you will. Apparently the years of lustfully tying each other to the bed, eating leftover Thai food, and falling asleep exhausted wearing nothing but Cheshire grins are over. Now we have to organize social activities that most often require wearing pants. I thought the sole purpose of being in a long-term relationship was not having to orchestrate such outings. Apparently, that is precisely why I've never been successful at long-term relationships.

My therapist is on board with the whole thing. She advises couples to date at least once a month. She calls it re-committing. I call it exhausting. First, there really aren't that many things I want to do, pants or not. Secondly, I prefer to be more spontaneous. At a moment's notice I want to be able to take (for example) an unscheduled nap. You can see how being locked into something written on a calendar would disrupt my impulsive, freewheeling lifestyle.

For me, a date is just the grown-up version of the "field trip," and I never liked those, either. You could count on a school-age Charlotte throwing up at the bus stop (often I didn't make it off my own front porch) on a field trip morning. Sometimes the permission slip alone made me retch. My mother said I had bad nerves and a field trip was simply beyond my limited emotional capacity. I think it had more to do with not wanting to waste a day touring Zug Island or the Henry Ford Museum only to drink warm Coke out of a can covered with aluminum foil. For the record, I'd like to know what Einstein came up with that method of refrigeration. As a result, I've never seen many of Detroit's historic sites—crime scenes, as the locals call them. Maybe one day I'll make my own bucket list of field trips I've missed. Probably not. That's what out-of-town guests are for.

My disinterest in most things makes dating that much harder. Since I loathe crowds and the majority of social functions, I have a journal filled with things I never want to do. Just say the words "Renaissance Festival" and watch my head explode.

At this point in my relationship with my partner, major undertakings like helicopters tours of the city and hot air balloon rides at sunset seem like way too much effort. I mean, come on, by now I'd like to think I've already got the girl. Who has $350 for helium?

A few years back I took Sharon on what I believe to be the ultimate date—a University of Michigan football game, replete with tailgate festivities, authorized collegiate apparel and a primer on the rules of the game. I brought a mini Nerf football. She brought a novel.

It's not that we're totally incompatible when it comes to dating. We are known to do the occasional dinner and a movie. Sometimes we even end up at the same theatre.

Most of our best dates haven't been preplanned. One evening Sharon gave me a tour of her childhood landmarks—elementary school, favorite aunt's house, the shop that made her school uniforms, the park where she fell off the swing and broke her pinkie finger. It was sweet and private and I got to know her in a new and more intimate way. I wouldn't trade that date for an opening night performance of *Die Fledermaus* no matter who was playing the role of the bat.

Under this new dating charter, Sharon and I are supposed to trade off scheduling duties to keep us both "vested" in the process. But for some reason managing a simple calendar that basically says "you/me/you/me" is also beyond my ability. As a result, she successfully tricks me into thinking it is always my turn to come up with the big dating plan.

Labor Pains

The upcoming Labor Day weekend was as vacant as an unplanted corn field. Looming on the horizon unscheduled bliss. Unfortunately, I was on the hook to create a romantic Hollywood moment. It was time for "the date."

I read in the local paper about an art festival being held in a nearby community. It fit all of my dating criteria: it was nearby, required no formal attire, promised food vendors, and the whole thing would be over in two hours tops. It had the added bonus of being free... or so I thought.

The event was held in the Village of Franklin, a quaint little burg about 15 miles northwest of Detroit. Founded in the 1820s, it is still known today as the "Town that Time Forgot." Franklin boasts a sleepy little cider mill, an old-fashioned tea room and an all-volunteer fire department. The 1,000 families that call the Village home love its cozy, homespun charm. They also love their multi-million dollar mansions and their six-figure median household incomes. The Village of Franklin is one part Plymouth Rock, five parts Beverly Hills. You'll find a lot more Manolo Blahniks on the cobblestone walkways of Franklin than you will colonial black-buckle flats.

It was a glorious day for our date. The smell of fresh baked pies and grilled Polish sausage wafted about the artist booths. All types of handiwork were represented in this virtual MasterCard commercial: Ceramic frog soap dispenser, $95. Photograph of wasp resting on day lily, $325. Wrought iron garden gnome, $395. Indonesian teak wood fruit bowl, $750 (fruit sold separately). Laughing at well-heeled stuffed shirts paying full price for all of this nonsense: Priceless.

Being comfortably unemployed, I felt safely insulated from any ridiculous buys. Fine art—even coarse art—was not atop my purchase funnel. I could pay my yearly home heating bill for what one man wanted for a hand-blown Christmas tree ornament. With three dogs and an unknown number of cats in our household, that decoration wouldn't last long enough to see baby New Year wet his first diaper.

I walked lazily, munched mindlessly and listened to a really bad Karaoke singer do his rendition of "All the Girls I've Loved Before" singing both the Willie Nelson and Julio Iglesias parts in their respective (and poorly executed) accents.

Our dog Faith came along to see for herself what all of this dating fuss was about. She was her usual good-natured self—waddling behind us without much interest in the whole proceeding. Like me, I believe she was just putting in her time until we could return to napping. So when she made a sudden, unexpected bee line for the booth marked #47 she startled me—nearly pulling me off my feet. Like my partner Sharon, once Faith has her mind set on something, she is unstoppable. While no one knows for sure, we believe Faith is part Chow, part North American Brown Bear and part Grand Master Jedi.

You Gotta Have Faith

Faith is another of our furry gifts from God. Some years ago, during the week preceding Christmas, Sharon found Faith frozen—quite literally—in a snow bank in our front yard. Sharon was leaving for work about 5:00 a.m. and noticed a dark motionless figure in the moonlight. The dog had no collar, tags, or (we learned later) tracking chip. It appeared she had run away or been abandoned—an unfortunate yet increasing practice in the land of Detroit-area home foreclosures.

It was several degrees below zero that morning. Sharon chipped the dog out of the ice and snow and immediately rushed her to an emergency veterinary clinic. The staff was able to revive the dog and found she was suffering from a number of health complications, including having just given birth. Upon hearing that tragic news, Sharon left the dog in the capable hands of the vet techs, tore home, and scoured the neighborhood for the next several hours, looking for a litter of puppies. None was found.

After two major surgeries and nearly a year of convalescence, we are blessed to report that Faith—aptly named by the vet techs during her ordeal—is now an integral member of our ever burgeoning pride. Once again, my beloved partner rescued an animal on the brink of death and found it a good home—ours.

Faith is definitely our beta dog (if there is such a thing), in the number two slot behind Sharon. She also holds the keys to our household's spirituality. This amazing dog has other-worldly abilities. It is no coincidence she was named Faith, or that she sought out Sharon that frigid morning. Much like St. Francis instructs, Faith brings joy and light and hope to everyone she meets.

Little Booth on the Prairie

Booth #47 stood out in stark contrast on the landscape of affluent artists. The artisan, Starphish Waverly, hailed from Oak Park—only 10 miles down the road from Franklin, but in a completely different economic stratosphere. Starphish was definitely not part of the Franklin Village inner circle, wearing what appeared to be a homemade smock, Simplicity pattern #3581.

Perhaps that's why Faith was drawn to her. Starphish had a peaceful and welcoming aura. She let me browse her wares without pressure. Her work spoke for itself— simple, authentic and every piece unique.

I liked it immediately. I liked her immediately. After some pleasant banter, I asked Starphish if she did special orders. I told her I'd been looking for a pendant—the iconic Alcoholics Anonymous triangle—to commemorate my five year sobriety anniversary. Since she was unfamiliar with the symbol, I drew a quick sketch. A less complex graphic you will not find. It is a triangle inside a circle. That's it. No special size, color, proportions or layout. You can't screw it up. That's what I love about AA—always trying to keep it simple.

The Perfect Triangle

The three-sided figure known as the triangle transcends time and is based on the perfection of the

259

number three. Everything comes in threes—Musketeers, deities (Father, Son, Holy Spirit), ring circuses, people in jokes (a rabbi, priest, and leprechaun walk into a bar), sports scoring (triple-double, hat trick), blind mice, little pigs, bears, stooges, Oriental kings, human birthing segments (trimesters) and dog nights.

Alcoholics Anonymous uses threes in many ways: to represent recovery, unity, and service; to define the disease concept of the body, mind, and spirit; to direct us to be honest, open, and willing; and to help us share our experience, strength, and hope. When the triangle is enclosed in a circle, it represents wholeness and oneness, ever reminding us we are not alone.

Starphish was a good sport about the whole thing—even congratulating me on my five years. She quoted me a modest price, took my e-mail address, and said she would contact me when the pendant was finished. She declined Sharon's offer of a deposit. It was a good old-fashioned handshake deal.

Blessed are the Meek

It was a rainy Sunday night, and Sharon and I were driving home from God knows where when it dawned on me that I still hadn't gotten my pendant. While only a week had passed, I was convinced I'd never see Starphish or her jewelry again.

"What a waste of time," I said in my usual judgmental tone. "She probably lost my number. She probably lost the drawing. You know how flaky artists are. I mean really, 'Starphish'? What kind of name is that?"

"It's only been a week," Sharon countered. "You'll hear from her."

The next morning—waiting for me in my digital inbox—was an email from Starphish telling me the piece was done. I immediately heard God laughing at me. I think He actually shot milk out of His nose.

For the record, I still think Starphish is a goofy name.

I picked the pendant up from her house later that week. It was beyond perfect; I couldn't have been more pleased. It was as if she had been making recovery jewelry all of her life. I admired myself holding the pendant in a vanity mirror; however, I wanted to hang it on a chain to get the full affect. Noticing the full scope of her workshop, I deduced Starphish had one or two necklaces hidden somewhere and so I asked. And she did.

"Do you want a 14- or 16- inch length?" she asked.

"I'm not sure, whatever you have will be great—I'm not very good at judging these things."

As Starphish opened miniature drawers and scanned her shelves, I began my usual blabbering—my personal mission to stamp out white space wherever it exists.

"You know, your house is probably less than a mile from my home group," I rattled on. "Every Sunday morning, there's a 12-step recovery meeting at the city's Community Center. Even though the rent is expensive, we meet there because Lord knows you can't find a church available for a Sunday morning meeting."

While continuing her quest for a silver chain, Starphish mumbled something barely audible beneath her breath.

"Yeah, my mom couldn't make it."

Nonplussed, I pressed on, telling her about my recovery and the details of my not so private life.

"I buy four dozen bagels for the meeting every Sunday morning. Cream cheese, too. Have been for more than four years now. If I don't show up on a Sunday morning, there are about 100 alcoholics ready to eat their Styrofoam cups and burn me in effigy. We alcoholics love our carbohydrates."

Starphish paused briefly, cocked her head and reiterated, "My mom wasn't able to go."

She tipped her chin to her chest and looked shyly away.

By now it was obvious even to me that Starphish had something to say; she just needed to do it in her own time. I waited. She put down the handfuls of stuff she had distractedly collected and said in almost a whisper, "My mother drank herself to death."

After more than five years in the program, I should know not to be surprised by anything. Not by what people do, not by their stories, not by the way God puts us together in seemingly coincidental situations. I shouldn't be, but I still am.

I quickly grabbed my two favorite tools from my ever present sobriety toolbox: the hug and the cry. I pulled Starphish close to me, held her tightly and began to cry. She responded in kind. After a multi-Kleenex embrace, I told her I was very sorry for her loss and for her mother's pain.

"That's okay," she said, producing a smile. "I have you now, and you're making it."

Doing the Holy Tango

God must feel like He's choreographing *Dancing with the Stars*, and we're all a bunch of morons learning our routines. He gets up early every morning, paints the numbered footprints on the ballroom floor, and tells us to keep our arms locked, our chins strong, and not to step on each other's feet. Every day it's the same lesson. It is the dance of God's will, and things always work out better when I let Him lead.

In the case of Starphish, our waltz had been many years in the making. It started when I put down the booze, bought a house in Pleasant Ridge and rescued my dog Tobi. The two of us became eight when we met a beautiful redhead and her brood at the community dog park. Then came Faith, who brought us to Starphish, whose mother died of the disease that nearly claimed my own life.

Through sharing our pain, Starphish and I were led to the sacred place of healing. Like the program tells me, all I have to be is honest, open and willing.

Somebody Get Me a Doctor

Healing is not anything I'm an expert on. Wounded—on that I could write a book. I believe that without healing, we are limited in our ability to do God's work. Seriously, how much good can I do the world if I'm living in an emotional dumpster, tracking garbage wherever I go?

Right now I'm reading an interesting book on healing by Louise Hay. The cover boasts that it's an "international best seller with more than 30 million copies sold worldwide." That in itself is a little healing. It's comforting to know that perhaps I'm not alone with my busted bones—that maybe we're all a little banged up. Maybe all of us have fallen out of the nest once or twice and need help mending our wings.

I'm Fucking Fine

Admitting we need help implies we're somewhat imperfect and our society doesn't do a great job with that message. We're never told that it's okay to get messy, fall down, miss the mark or ask for help. And so we grow into frightened people who are terrified to admit we don't have all the answers.

Because we won't reach out for help, God has to paint the footprints on the floor. He helps us get from the liquor store to the 12-step meeting; from the dog park to the art booth. He puts us with dance partners who need to learn the same routines. And when we do, amazing things happen.

Since that day in her living room, Starphish and I have exchanged notes about the mystery of our encounter. Her mother's story will be a constant reminder of the gift of my sobriety. She said she had love in her heart for my courage. No one has ever said anything like that to me. Ever.

I asked my therapist Diane about healing and if she thought it was truly possible. She is among the most amazing, gifted and spiritual people I know. I figured if anybody had the answer, she did.

"Healing is a process of changing our patterns," she said. "It's about forgiveness, release and love. Not only for others, but for ourselves."

Fall on Your Knees

My knees look like poorly carved holiday hams. They grotesquely display every stupid, clumsy thing I've ever done. I've fallen off motorcycles, bicycles, skateboards and shopping carts. In marching band I knocked over an entire drum line and took out a sizable chunk of the school's football field. You name it, I've tripped over it, ran into it or landed on top of it. I'm a one-person wrecking ball; a "klutz" as my dad lovingly called me. I should wear a crash helmet just to take in the mail. Doctors in the neighboring ER know me by my first name and blood type.

Despite being somewhat disfigured, I'm glad to report that I've recuperated from all of my injuries. Considering some 50 years of wear and tear, I'm able-bodied and ambulatory. I can still pedal my bike and walk the dogs and dance with the woman I love.

Maybe that's what healing is. Having the tell-tale scars of our woundedness but no longer feeling the pain. Remembering our mistakes and choosing to do life a little differently. Today, I know that no matter how much something might hurt, the pain will eventually subside. And when it does, I'll be that much wiser and more able to do God's work.

As St. Francis said, it is in forgiving I am forgiven. In releasing I am set free. And while I'm certainly no Julianne Hough, today I can dance with God, and no one (usually) gets hurt.

TLL

Dude Looks Like a Lady

I'll be the first to admit, I'm not an expert on most things. In fact, not a single thing jumps to mind. My actual lack of expertise is somewhat renowned within a segment of our society titled, "Jobs," subtitled, "Paid." Some might call me a master in the art of napping. I'm skilled at feeding cats with chopsticks. If FOX News ever needed someone on set to debate the controversial issue of Thanksgiving side dishes, I'm quite confident I could pull it off respectfully. Lord knows the number of arguments I've had over the years with my father on the topic of cranberries: Me supporting the full-berried chutney version; him on the side of jellied and slithering from a can.

There are many sources for expert advice in today's digital society. Rather than ask me, I advise people to consult the infinite universe of content located on wiki/snap/tube/twit/yelp/pin/plus. I'm pretty sure it's a thing. Siri is also a knowledgeable repository of information and is always eager to please.

Despite my attempts to deflect such inquiries, I'm frequently assaulted with questions on the broad topic I'll call "gay." I guess, based on a number of tells, including a summer wardrobe that consists mainly of

1960s-era gym shorts from various U.S. colleges and universities, people think I'm gay. I've become the *Encyclopedia Britannica* for straight people bursting with curiosity about us strange and magnificent birds. Lord knows we've given them enough fodder. This year alone the poor dears have been inundated with headlines that simply don't compute in their binary little brains.

These breeders ask me about same-sex marriage, Bruce/Caitlyn Jenner, and if the goaltender for the German Women's Soccer Team is, indeed, a woman. I feel bad. Not because of the annoying and seemingly endless interrogatives, but because I have nothing of value to offer them. Unfortunately, I have no rainbow-colored key card to unlock the mysteries of gay culture, mating or pageantry. I cannot quench their thirst for knowledge with a sip from my hers-and-hers font of wisdom.

I am gay, but as my partner will attest, I'm certainly no expert at it. People shouldn't miss this very important distinction: Just because a person *does* a particular thing does not necessarily elevate that person to expert status. Any number of politicians come to mind, along with actors, writers, professional athletes and my former dentist. Does anyone really want career advice from Anthony Weiner? Acting lessons from Ashton Kutcher? Ethics in journalism from Brian Williams? Of course not. These people aren't experts; they're negligent practitioners at best.

Many in our society are eager to position themselves as authorities on any subject, whether they are or aren't. To them, it doesn't seem to matter either way. Give them the opportunity and they'll bloviate till complete exhaustion—theirs and yours. My ex-husband had a boss who was infamous for the line, "I don't know what I'm saying, but I will tell you this." At least the buffoon was honest.

Ignorance is Bliss

Despite my lack of any real merit, I've become a kind of lesbian decoder ring for my befuddled straight friends.

"Why do you keep asking me?" I whine in response to their constant barrage of questions.

I don't know:

> • If man who transgenders to female but is attracted to women is called a lesbian.
>
> • If a lesbian that had been married to another woman in the state of Vermont prior to the Supreme Court Ruling on same sex marriage, but who now wants to marry a different woman in the state of Michigan (where same-sex marriage was previously illegal but now is) first needs to divorce woman #1, or how that process actually works.
>
> • If Bruce Jenner's surgery was covered under Obamacare. Or if his children should send him cards on Mother's Day or Father's Day.

- If there are now more than two genders. Or what exactly the terms gender queer and pansexuality mean.
- Why the U.S. continues to do business with nations that slaughter their gays and lesbians like Perdue chickens. Or if half of the Republican candidates that ran for president in 2016—if elected—wouldn't try to legalize homosexual genocide here as well.
- What the acronym LGBTQIA means, or if it's really just a 6-year old attempting to recite the alphabet for the first time.

If you are uninitiated like me, you think QUILTBAG is a satchel for toting around one's yarn and pinking shears. Not so, according to queerumich.com. The letters describe the University of Michigan's confusingly diverse yet inclusive coed community, using "queer as an umbrella term for bisexual, transgender, lesbian, same-gender-long, questioning, asexual, gay, non-labeling and anyone not heterosexual or 'cisgender.'" I remember when the student body referred to themselves as wolverines or simply, "superior in all ways."

My parents were shocked to learn that both boys and girls occupied many of the same dormitories at Michigan State in 1981. I'm quite confident I would have been yanked out of East Lansing had they known young men and women with perversions such as these were roaming the campus freely. Or worse yet, that I was one of them.

Bruce Almighty

There is nothing that can, or should, be said about Caitlyn Jenner that hasn't been said already. The poor dear has been analyzed, scrutinized, judged, maligned, examined and inspected from every angle. And, again, by people without a speck of credibility. I'll concede that she's created much of the hoopla. She's fueled an international frenzy; baiting tabloids with photo shoots, primetime interviews and reality shows. But I've never heard of anyone being arrested for being a media whore. If so, most of Hollywood would be serving a life sentence.

Maybe it's in Caitlyn's nature to "out publicity" the Kardashian clan. She was, after all (as her anatomical/hormonal former self) named the "World's Greatest Athlete," earning a gold medal in the grueling decathlon event at the 1976 Montreal Olympic Games. I guess you can take the man out of the man, but maybe not the fierce competitive drive.

I really don't know why Caitlyn's version of a modern-day woman is being played out as a 1950's sex kitten. The 65-year-old's *Vanity Fair* cover is more Marilyn Monroe than Hilary Clinton. I'm not saying that all accomplished women in 2016 need to look like Ruth Bader Ginsburg. Caitlyn is free to live life as the iconic pin-up woman of her/his dreams. Is she driving the feminists wild? Absolutely. Does she look any more or less like Madonna or Cher attempting to turn back time? Absolutely not. Is she more fixated on stereotypical female trappings than she should be? Who's to judge?

Certainly not me. I can't put on eyeliner without looking like Marilyn Manson. Russell Brand, Steven Tyler and Miss Piggy wear more makeup than most of the lesbians I know. Except for my partner, who won't leave the house without foundation and mascara. Not even to install a new radiator in her Jeep. Now that I think about it, no wonder all the straights are confused.

Guess Who's Coming to Dinner?

This is how bad I am at solving gender's Rubik's Cube:

I pursued my partner relentlessly over a period of several months before she finally agreed to go out with me. During that time, I asked a number of people—people I believed to be her intimates—if Sharon was gay. No one was certain. They argued both for and against. The usual lesbian cues weren't present—no flannel, no big ring-o-keys attached to her dungarees, no asymmetric and over gelled "Flock of Seagulls" hair do.

I met Sharon at our community dog park. At first glance, she took my breath away. She possessed an alluring self-assurance and quiet strength. While I ran from person to person seeking emotional pats on the head, Sharon often brought a thick book and sat alone at a picnic table far from the human/canine fray. Each time I approached her with my ill-behaved dog and overly aggressive "hellos" she recoiled a bit. She was much like her dog: Detached, aloof and bordering on disdainful. She was a sexual enigma; I was determined to break her code.

After my eighth petition, Sharon finally surrendered, accepting my invitation to go "out." As she delights in telling people, she was caught off guard (indeed I had intercepted her on her daily run—but not in the stalkerish way it sounds). We agreed she would pick me up for dinner that Friday at 8:00 p.m.

It Was Only Tuesday

I was delighted—she was my white whale and I her Ishmael. But in a moment my euphoria turned to dread: Were we having dinner? Or was this a date?

When I retell this story, especially to straight girls, most can sympathize. They invariably know that if asked out by a man, it is no doubt for the purpose of sex. If dining with another gal, no below the belt action is implied.

Here was my dilemma: Were Sharon and I two new friends simply going out for supper? Or was this a date, and with it all of the implications thereof?

To me, date implies something much different than dining with friends—male or female. First there is the appearance requirement. I would never spend hours preening for friends. They're lucky if I show up freshly bathed and wearing clothes not slept on by cats. I eat with abandon. I get food on my shirt. When the check comes, I can't be found. I'm a slightly smelly, mostly ill-mannered and overly affectionate doggie dining companion who'll wolf down my food and yours too if not properly guarded.

Up until July 14, 2006, the night of this yet to be defined "dinner," I had not dated since—possibly ever. I am not a dater. In my past "relationships," s/he and I were friends before accidentally having sex. There was none of the usual cat-and-mouse pursuit that accompanies what I imagine to be dating. I had become a stranger in a strange land and I didn't like it.

For the days preceding Friday at 8:00 p.m., I hounded my friends. Much like the confused baby bird in the children's book, *Are You My Mother*, I inquired relentlessly, "Do you think this is a date?" I was not popular with my friends that week.

"You are the worst lesbian ever," was their usual response. "How can you not tell if you're going on a date?"

I was the worst lesbian ever. And I'm still no expert today.

The anguish built into a paralysis of anxiety.

"I can't go," I finally proclaimed to my recovery mentor. "I just can't do it."

"You are an absolute ass," she said. It was her usual retort. "You have succeeded in scheduling time with a person you find interesting and would like to get to know better, and your best thinking is to cancel."

"But I don't want to make a fool of myself," I said. "What if I do something stupid?"

"Of course you're going to do something stupid, you're you. But that aside, did it ever occur to you that at this point, it doesn't matter either way—straight or gay. You're just making a new friend. Your intent should not be to bed her tonight, or profess your undying love from atop a U-Haul. Slow down. It's one meal. What if you have nothing in common or she turns out to be a serial killer?"

Dress to (Un)impress

Of course I hadn't considered any of that. We were simply two people sharing an hour or two of time. That was the blessing. A miracle, really. Her advice was to let go and let God take the wheel. While she was right, there was still the awkward issue of attire: Dress too casually and telegraph the wrong message to a potential life partner. Try to look sexy, and risk giving a nice straight girl nightmares for months.

In the end, I chose khakis and a breezy cotton T-shirt, which is the perfect asexual outfit. Her dress was more revealing—literally and figuratively. She had exchanged her usual baseball cap and running shoes for a black camisole and butt-hugging slacks. Instead of the well-worn Jeep Wrangler she drove to the dog park, she arrived at my home in a sleek black Lexus. She drove us to Ann Arbor where we ate at a rather romantic pan-Asian restaurant. I was so nervous that I nearly impaled her with one of my chopsticks. In my defense, they were metal and very slippery.

275

As the evening unfolded, we talked and laughed and exchanged life stories, bite by delicious bite. I found Sharon to be kind and smart and extremely well mannered. Unbeknown to me at the time, I was starting a beautiful friendship with the woman who would eventually share my world.

I learned a lot that night about expectations and labels, the delight in maintaining a bit of mystery and the great joy that can come from giving up control. We all deserve the chance to be discovered from the inside out. I so often let the wrapper get in the way. An individual's outward appearance, I've learned living in one of America's "gayest" communities, is hardly an indicator of one's true nature, least of all sexual identity. Today I try very hard to restrain myself from judging a book by its black, white or rainbow-colored cover.

The Package

What defines male and female? Straight and gay? Curious, but perhaps not that curious?

One of my dearest female friends has only one breast; cancer claimed the other. She continues to identify as a woman. So does Angelina Jolie, who has neither breasts nor ovaries. My very heterosexual uncle Phil has two massive boobs that could rival Dolly Parton's. A day at the beach with him is no day at the beach. Despite being born with a bosom, Chaz (formerly Chastity) Bono now resembles the late Sonny more than his mom.

276

To quote a famous poultry philosopher: "Parts is parts."

On its website, The Philadelphia Center for Transgender Surgery posts a price list for the various procedures it offers. The cost of a fully functioning penis: $50,000. I know a lot of women who'd like to buy one of those for their marginally functioning husband. Vaginoplasty, including a penile inversion, clitoroplasty and labiaplasty, is roughly half the price.

For less than the price of a new Toyota Camry, any man can trade his "pre-owned" penis for a shiny new vagina. If you want the premium package—from Adam's apple to caboose—be ready to shell out Mercedes money. For the right price, any part is yours for the taking. You can be your own Mr. or Mrs. Potato Head of genitalia.

I'm joking when I shouldn't. An individual's gender identification is an extremely serious, personal and potentially painful exploration. No one needs my, or anyone else's, opinion mucking up the mix. Caitlyn, and others like her, deserve respect, support and privacy, even when they don't ask for it.

A number of gay folks are on record demeaning the transgender population. Like having sex with someone of the same sex is just dandy, but anything beyond that is just too weird. Please. Just because I don't want a penis doesn't give me the right to disparage another woman who might. The LGBT community of tidy glass houses should know better than to start pitching stones. If for no other reason, we all throw like girls.

277

Any group of people that has ever been marginalized is duty bound to support another without exception—black, Jew, LGBT, disabled, elderly or other. A single class cannot win its freedom on the backs of others and then abandon the fight. We must remember Pastor Marin Niemöller's haunting words:

First they came for the Socialists,
and I did not speak out—
because I was not a Socialist.
Then they came for the Jews,
and I did not speak out—
because I was not a Jew.
Then they came for me—
and there was no one left to speak for me.

What's That Middle Thing?

Some experts regard the growing exploration of sexual ambiguity, especially among young people, the natural outcome of society's overly rigid and prescriptive gender definitions. Our long-held male/female archetypes are being challenged and with cause. Really, is the embodiment of the homogametic sex really best represented by a Victoria Secret model? And the male version currently starring in the latest Thor movie?

Many kids of this generation have the courage to rage against the gender machine. They are the 2016 versions of '80s gender benders Prince, David Bowie and Annie Lennox. Their refusal to package their sexual identity into one of two pre-assembled boxes flips a middle finger at the traditional boy/girl paradigm.

They are not alone. All types of experts are now referring to gender binarism as only one type of gender system. Other systems, considered less divisive and polarizing, are gaining traction among academics and sexologists. Yes, that's also a thing. Brown University professor Anne Fausto-Sterling suggests adding three more gender categories in her paper, "The Five Sexes: Why Male and Female Are Not Enough." I've been told that eight is enough, but that was back in the '70s.

The German Judge Gives Me a 5.95

Nearly 70 years ago Alfred Kinsey developed a six-point scale to determine a person's sexual identify. Zero, on the one end, is for people who identify exclusively as heterosexuals. Six, on the other, means 100-percent pure Grade A gay. Kinsey kindly offers the numbers 1-5 for the folks who like a bit of both. Kinsey was an early detractor of gender binarism and believed neither male nor female represented two discrete populations, but rather a continuum of sexual orientation, which can change over time.

Kinsey's work provided the building blocks for those still attempting to codify sexual identity with surgical accuracy. In *Breaking Through the Binary*, Sam Killermann tries to decipher the nuances of gender using four criteria:

- Gender identity: Who you think you are. Do you fit better into the societal role of "woman" or "man," or does neither ring true for you?
- Gender expression: Demonstrating gender through your dress, behavior and interactions.
- Biological sex: Your organs, hormones and chromosomes.
- Sexual orientation: Who you are physically, spiritually, and emotionally attracted to.

For me, this theory only muddies the water. Each of these categories presents a host of exceptions and caveats and possibilities requiring further exploration. Killermann admits it himself, writing:

"There's much more to attraction than sexuality. Pansexuals experience attraction without gender as a factor. If you experience romantic attraction but not sexual, you might identify as asexual or—depending on the gender(s) you're attracted to—hetero-, homo- or panromantic. If you're attracted to folks who are trans or androgynous, you might identify as skoliosexual."

Then there's the issue of intersex, formerly known as hermaphrodite (which is no longer a PC word). Everything I know about this category I learned from Jeffrey Eugendies and my book club in 2003. It goes without saying I know very little about this category.

Ultimately, Killermann believes that a person's sexual orientation doesn't determine their gender expression. And their gender expression isn't determined by their gender identity. And their gender identity isn't determined by their biological sex.

So what's the point? And why are we spending so much time trying to figure this stuff out? To quote today's youth, "WTF?"

Are we evolving or devolving into a genderless society? Are we taking something once so seemingly simple and endlessly complicating it, as humans are oft to do? Aren't the requisite female/male gender roles necessary for our species to survive?

Does anyone still want to be Carol Brady or Marion Cunningham or June Cleaver? Maybe Caitlyn does. God bless her for that.

Doggie Style

My partner and I maintain a household with numerous pets. Among them, three dogs, all of which would blend in perfectly at the intergalactic cantina featured in *The Empire Strikes Back*. They are strange, Wookie-like beasts of unknown origin or species. For the most part, we consider them peaceful aliens with strange customs, including a preoccupation with their nether regions.

In an attempt to satisfy their insatiable appetites, I recently scoured the shelves of my local pet emporium for low-fat snacks and came upon a fancy box labeled,

"Canine Heritage." Its slogan read: "Fill in the Missing Pieces with Canine Heritage™ Breed Test, the first DNA-based test to determine the composition of your mixed-breed dog."

The ingenious folks at Canine Heritage have devised a genetic identification system whereby with a simple mouth swab I can—within four to six weeks—learn the "potential breeds" contained within my mutt's questionable lineage. It's like ancestory.com for canines. Armed with this data I, the concerned and inquisitive "pet parent," am told I can provide my pet a better life (like that's possible). This includes the ability to prepare a breed-specific diet and exercise plan, spot potential health risks and better understand my dog's unique behaviors.

Unfortunately, there is a major flaw in Canine Heritage's marketing premise. Neither my partner nor I have any desire to learn more about our pets. Alas, I have no unsatisfied curiosities about the four-legged creatures that live among us with flatulence issues and a constant desire to invade our bed. Learning more about my dog Tobi, for example, will not improve our pet/parent bond. We know too much about each other as it is. The mystery went out of our relationship the day I picked up his poop and realized much too late that the fresh-scented, overpriced sanitation bag I was using had not been properly sealed at one very important end. He's watched me flounder with feminine hygiene products. We take the same thyroid medicine and have been caught alternating licks from the same ice-cream cone. I wake up spooning him or with him spooning me. We have the same hair color. I pay big money for it.

I'm certainly no expert, but I cannot think of one aspect of our relationship that would be improved by my learning Tobi's sordid genealogy. His mother was a tramp—enough said.

What would it matter if I learned that one of my so-called dogs was 72 percent Tibetan Mastiff or 58 percent Welsh Corgi or 3 percent Catahoula Leopard Dog? Would I like them more or less? Would they have greater value? Would I give that "special one" artesian water or Kobe beef or even more space in the bed?

Would I feel shame for the one mixed with Pit Bull or Chow? Would I not include that one on walks for fear of being seen out in my community? Would I return that one very mixed-up mixed breed to the pound to be euthanized?

Would my feelings abruptly change upon learning something as unimportant and inconsequential *as that*? The answer is a resounding, "No!"

I'm pretty sure that's the lesson. Unconditional love is unconditional—nothing else matters. Not who you love or what you wear or what's going on between your ears or your legs. And that goes double if you're a Yorkie-doodle with ambiguous genitalia and a red-hot crush on the Peekapug that lives next door.

TLL

About the Author

Charlotte Fisher (b. 1963) began her writing career passing notes in the 7th grade. Since then, she's worked as a journalist, dog walker, greeting card writer and in corporate communications. Based in the Detroit area, her non-fiction work is largely biographical, focusing on sobriety, spirituality, healing and hope. Fisher shares her tragic, comedic, tender and twisted stories with the goal of helping others, having learned that, "Our pain is our greatest gift." She credits writers Anne Lamott and Erma Bombeck for their ability to find humor in adversity and wisdom in everyday life.

At a time when she believed such things mattered, Fisher received her BA in Journalism from Michigan State University and MBA from The University of Michigan. She is most proud of her recovery, her service work and the rescue animals she shares with her partner of more than a decade. She also spends a lot of time napping and watching YouTube cat videos. Her sobriety date is March 23, 2004.

Find her on Facebook and at lesbianlunch.com.

Made in the USA
Charleston, SC
04 January 2017